Easy
Tasty
Cheap

First published in Great Britain in 2025 by
Hamlyn, an imprint of
Octopus Publishing Group Ltd
Carmelite House
50 Victoria Embankment
London EC4Y 0DZ
www.octopusbooks.co.uk

An Hachette UK Company
www.hachette.co.uk

The authorized representative in the EEA is
Hachette Ireland, 8 Castlecourt Centre, Dublin
15, D15 XTP3, Ireland (email: info@hbgi.ie)

Copyright © Octopus Publishing Group 2025

Distributed in the US by Hachette Book Group
1290 Avenue of the Americas, 4th and 5th Floors
New York, NY 10104

Distributed in Canada by Canadian Manda Group
664 Annette St., Toronto, Ontario,
Canada, M6S 2C8

ISBN 978-0-600-63917-6

A CIP catalogue record for this book is available
from the British Library.

Printed and bound in China.

10 9 8 7 6 5 4 3 2 1

Publisher: Lucy Pessell
Designer: Isobel Platt
Senior Editor: Tim Leng
Assistant Editor: Samina Rahman
Production Manager: Caroline Alberti
Illustrations: Isobel Platt

Picture Acknowledgements
Photography: Octopus Publishing Group
Additional photography: Dreamstime.com:
Bogdan Wańkowicz 32, Olha Afanasieva 21;
iStock: 5second 27, Anna_Shepulova 65, Cavan
Images 84, DronG 63, HandmadePictures 90,
haoliang 122, KirstenFowle 22, LauriPatterson
168, Mizina 24, Olga Mazyarkina 43, vaaseenaa
57, zkruger 55.

Disclaimer: The recipes in this book have
been labelled if suitable for Vegan and
Vegetarian diets. Vegetarians should look
for the 'V' symbol on a cheese to ensure it
is made with vegetarian rennet.

MIX
Paper | Supporting
responsible forestry
FSC
www.fsc.org   FSC® C008047

Easy Tasty Cheap

The ultimate student cookbook

Thalia Rhodes

hamlyn

Contents

One Pot

Great meals made easy – just throw all your ingredients in one pot and cook up a storm.

Speedy Meals

Perfect recipes for when you're living in the fast lane but still want great tasting food.

Hangover and Comfort Food

Perfect food for the morning after the night before, or simply when you need a big foody hug.

Batch Cooking

Save time and effort by cooking in batches – future you will thank you.

Food to Impress

Date night, mates coming over, or family visiting – these are the recipes that are sure to impress.

Sweet Treats

Everyone deserves a little treat now and again, so why not try these indulgent recipes?

INTRODUCTION

There's way more to student cooking than beans, breakfast cereal and biscuits. With the help of this easy-to-follow book you'll pick up a few culinary skills, learn to experiment in the kitchen and enjoy some great home-cooking along the way.

There are over 200 easy, tasty and cheap recipes for everyone, from curries and cakes to comfort food and casseroles – plus recipes to impress, meals that will fuel your brain and great one-pot wonders.

Once you have some confidence in the kitchen, you can tweak the recipes and will know how to knock up a pasta dish with whatever is on hand in the freezer or use leftover veg, a can of pulses and a stock cube as the basis of a simple and filling winter-warming soup. And remember, if you have eggs, you have a meal, be it a fried egg on toast or a fluffy omelette.

Make it Easy

Anyone can cook – just be sure to read the recipe through before you begin and make sure you have all the ingredients to hand. Get to grips with some basic cookery terminology below and check out the list of essential equipment and you are ready to start.

Cookery terms

Al dente: Cooked just long enough so still firm to the bite.

Baste: This means brushing food with oil or marinade while it is cooking to keep it moist and add flavour.

Cream: This term is used in baking and means beating the butter or spread with sugar using a wooden spoon (or electric mixer, if you are lucky enough to have one) until it is a pale colour and creamy smooth.

Fold: Folding is gently mixing in while keeping as much air in the mixture as possible. It's particularly important in some cake recipes for a light result.

Marinate: A way of getting extra flavour into fish, meat or chicken by leaving it to soak in a sauce – for example, jerk seasoning or a mix of olive oil and lemon – before cooking.

Season: This means adding salt and pepper, though sometimes a recipe will say to season with spices or lemon juice. The trick is to add a little at a time and taste as you go along.

Simmer: To cook over a low heat so that bubbles break the surface.

Stir-fry: To cook thinly sliced veg and meat or fish in a little oil in a wok or large frying pan for just few minutes, stirring all the time for even cooking.

Essential equipment

If you're starting from scratch you'll probably have to beg or borrow most of your kitchen equipment, which means you won't be cooking with state-of-the-art pans and processors. But you don't actually need many gadgets to rustle up any of the recipes in this book. With just a few basics you can eat well and even impress your friends with more dazzling creations when you develop some culinary confidence. Here's a list of the equipment you'll need:

Utensils: Measuring jug, two different-sized mixing bowls, wooden spoon, rolling pin, grater, spatula, chopping board, vegetable peeler, whisk, colander, sharp knives (one small for prepping veg and one large for chopping, slicing bread etc).

Pots and pans: Large and small saucepan (with lids), large nonstick frying pan, steamer (very useful but a metal colander over a pan will work fine). A wok is also handy for quick stir-fries, and can be used as an alternative to other pans.

Cookware: Baking sheet, roasting tin, flameproof casserole dish, large rectangular ovenproof dish (for lasagnes, bakes etc), wire cooling rack, cake tins, muffin tin and pastry cutters (if you're a baker).

A blender or food processor: This is a luxury item that will prove useful if you find your cooking mojo. But don't worry if you can't get your hands on these pricier pieces of culinary kit – a relatively inexpensive hand blender will do the job for most soups and smoothies and your knife skills will be all the better for chopping everything by hand.

Prep & cook times

You'll need to have some idea how long it will be until dinner's on the table, so each recipe is marked with a handy symbol:

<20 = 20 minutes and under

>20 = 20+ minutes

>50 = 50+ minutes

How do I know if it's cooked?

Ovens should be preheated to the specific temperature – if using a fan-assisted oven, follow manufacturer's instructions for adjusting the time and the temperature.

Chicken, turkey and pork must be thoroughly cooked before serving. To test whether meat and poultry are cooked, insert a skewer or thin-bladed knife into the thickest part of the meat. For a whole chicken, skewer through the thickest part of the drumstick or into the breast meat and then wait a few seconds – if the juices run clear, it is ready. If there are any traces of pink, then it needs a little longer. Cook for 10 minutes more, then test again. For pork chops or a joint of pork, insert the skewer into the centre, then check the meat juices in the same way.

Beef and lamb can be eaten slightly pink, according to your personal preference.

Fish is cooked through when it is the same colour all the way through and the flesh breaks easily into flakes. Uncooked prawns will turn pink all over when cooked through.

Measurements

Both imperial and metric measurements have been given in all recipes. Use one set of measurements only and not a mixture of both.

Standard level spoon measurement are used in all recipes.

1 tablespoon = one 15 ml spoon
1 teaspoon = one 5 ml spoon

Make it Tasty

Below is a list of basic staples for boosting flavour but you can gradually build up a stock of your favourite spices and ingredients for the dishes you turn to often.

Stock up your store cupboard

Your first grocery shop will probably be the most expensive, as you'll need to stock up on store cupboard essentials that form the basis of many meals. Alternatively, as with equipment, you could devise a list and ask everyone to bring a few items when you move in.

Condiments: Salt and pepper are essential for many recipes and good seasoning will liven up most dishes (unless otherwise stated, pepper used in the recipes in this book should be freshly ground black pepper). You will also need vegetable oil or olive oil for cooking and extra virgin olive oil for dressings and sauces. Ketchup, mayonnaise and mustard are also staples and there are some great vegan versions available.

Butter or spread: Toast is a student staple so a good supply of butter or spread – dairy-free if you are vegan – is essential. This is also an important ingredient for mash.

Spices: You don't need a full range of spices in a student kitchen but if you stock up on chilli powder, turmeric, cumin and maybe some mustard and fennel seeds, you'll be able to rustle up a half decent curry. Stock cubes and bouillon powders are also handy when you don't have any fresh stock made up (see page 197).

Onions and garlic: Like salt and pepper, onion and garlic are vital ingredients in all manner of dishes across all cuisines. These have a long shelf life if you keep them in the fridge.

Pasta and rice: Bakes, salads, risottos, curries, soups, pilafs...the list is endless and a good stock of pasta and rice will see you through the lean times.

Pulses and grains: Split peas, lentils, couscous, bulgar wheat and quinoa are fantastic store cupboard staples for meals in their own right, or used to bulk up soups and stews.

Cans: Cans of beans (kidney beans, butter beans and so on), sweetcorn and chickpeas are dependable favourites when the budget is suffering. They are cheap and nutritious and can be swiftly turned into a curry or chilli with a few additional ingredients.

Cheese: Put it in a sandwich, melt it on toast, add it to a burger or simply grate it over pasta, cheese can make so many meals taste even better. There are also vegetarian and vegan forms of Parmesan, Feta, Cheddar, Cheshire, Red Leicester, Dolcelatte and many goats' cheeses, among others.

Freezer staples: A lot of student accommodation suffers from the lack of a decent freezer and you might have to make do with a couple of shelves or a small compartment at the top of the fridge. But as long as there's space for some frozen vegetables and a few tubs of leftovers you should be able to get by.

Make it Cheap

You'll need to be organized when it comes to budgeting and shopping for food. If you're moving in with people you already know then it makes sense to work out what kitchen equipment you'll need and divide the list between you. That way, you won't end up with six juicers and an empty crockery cupboard. Likewise, when it comes to shopping, your budget will stretch much further if you pool your resources and shop as a household. You can buy ingredients in bulk and make the most of buy-one-get-one-free deals. However, you'll need to take individual preferences and diets into account – it's hardly fair if the vegetarian among you has to fund a weekly meat feast.

Food can be a cause of tension in shared houses so it's a good idea to set out a few simple rules when you first move in. That doesn't mean installing CCTV in the fridge and keeping your favourite cereal in a safe. But it does mean working out a cooking and shopping rota, if you're going to eat meals together. You'll need to decide on a feasible weekly food budget and allocate someone to take control of it. You obviously won't all be eating at home every night of the week so you could, for example, club together for midweek meals and then let everyone fend for themselves at the weekend.

Costing

To help you budget, each recipe in this book is given a rating of **£**, **££** or **£££**. The ones marked **£** are your go-to recipes for when funds are low. At the other end of the scale, **£££** marks the recipes ideal for those 'I deserve a treat' occasions.

Savvy shopping

To help you stick to your budget, it pays to shop wisely.

Make a list and stick to it: Before leaving for the supermarket, make a list of the things you need. When you get there, make sure you only buy what's on the list and nothing else. Don't be tempted to buy items on impulse just because they catch your eye.

Don't buy more than you can afford or than you can eat while it is still fresh – it's a good idea to take cash with you, and only enough to cover what you need to buy so you can't spend any more.

Don't go shopping when you're hungry either, or you'll end up with unnecessary items going through the checkout!

Check out market stalls and farmers' markets as you may find cheap fruit and veg there.

Pick up supermarket bargains towards closing time when items are being discounted! Also, look out for special offers, such as buy-one-get-one-free, at the supermarket, but only buy them if they are things you will actually eat, otherwise they will be wasted.

Bulk cooking

Another way to save money is to do your cooking in bulk. Just make a bit extra and put it in the freezer until needed. Don't forget to stock up on some freezer bags or containers, aluminium foil and foil trays to store all your food as individual portions. Good options for bulk cooking include curries, stews, chillies, pasta sauces and soups.

You can also freeze small portions of homemade stock in ice cube trays. It's easy then to just take out one at a time to use in your soups and stews – you don't even need to defrost them.

See page 5 for some other great ideas for batch cooking.

Love leftovers

'Waste not, want not'. With a little imagination, today's leftovers can be made into tomorrow's feast. Cooked cold pasta, roasted veg and potatoes can form the basis of salads and tortillas, vegetables can be added to homemade soups or pasta sauces, a few spoons of last night's curry or bolognese sauce will transform a baked potato. Mashed potato could be used to make bubble and squeak, hash browns or fish cakes.

Make it Healthy

Leaving home and living on your own can be both challenging and exciting. And while you're busy settling in and meeting new people, food can swiftly slide down the list of priorities. But it's important to establish good habits from the beginning and try to incorporate healthy eating as part of a healthy lifestyle. It's no more expensive or time consuming to eat healthily – it just takes a bit more planning. So, if you want to enjoy a varied diet that doesn't have to be emptied on to your plate from a microwave tub, it's time to up your game in the kitchen.

Five a day

It's common knowledge that we should all aim to eat at least five portions of fresh fruit and vegetables every day but it's easy to lose track. However, if you want to stay healthy, this is a quick and easy way to cram plenty of vitamins and minerals into your diet.

High five

1. Get in the habit of having fruit with breakfast and you've already earned one of your five before you leave the house – this could be chopped fruit on muesli or granola, a glass of fresh juice, or a banana on your cornflakes or porridge.

2. Steam vegetables as an accompaniment to dinner or have a side salad.

3. Switch your usual mid-morning bag of crisps for some chopped carrots and hummus.

4. Try ordering a fruit smoothie instead of that double-shot latte – you'll get the same buzz while upping your daily dose of fruit.

5. Tuck into a baked potato or toast piled high with baked beans – pulses count as one portion so there's no need to miss out on a lunchtime fave.

Healthy habits

It's easy to get into bad habits when you're responsible for all your own food shopping and meal prep. You might have the best intentions about staying healthy and eating a nutritious and balanced diet, but when you're dashing straight from the lecture theatre to the pub, or you're craving a sugar hit to get you through a marathon essay-writing session, it's easy to fall off the wellbeing wagon and reach for salty snacks, energy drinks and chocolate bars.

Sugar rush

Sugar offers a short-term solution to lethargy but it won't keep you company for very long, as the initial buzz is swiftly followed by an energy lapse and a craving for more sugary junk food. It's the added sugars in food and drink that are the real enemy, especially if the food doesn't have any other redeeming nutritional features. So always check the label to see just how much sugar the product contains and to give yourself a reality check and a nudge to choose a healthier alternative.

Fizzy drinks, processed snacks, some breakfast cereals and pasta sauces are all major culprits, but making simple changes like switching to porridge for breakfast, making your own sauce and cutting out the unnecessary biscuits and chocolate bars can all make a big difference. And do you really need two or three spoons of sugar in your morning coffee? Think of added sugar as empty calories – something your body doesn't need and something you can easily train it not to crave.

Call time on drinking

A healthy lifestyle doesn't mean you have to treat your body like a temple 24/7. It's all about balance and making sensible choices most of the time. As long as you're aware of what you should be eating and drinking, the odd splurge or treat isn't the end of the world.

The same is true for drinking. Know your limitations and be aware of the number of units you're drinking. They can quickly add up, even during the more innocuous evenings in the pub. So, if you're out a few times a week, you're likely to be drinking far more than the recommended government guidelines, which are to drink no more than 14 units per week and to have several alcohol-free days every week.

Know your units

One unit is 10 ml or 8 g of pure alcohol. This is a quick guide to how many units are in your favourite drink:

Small shot of spirits (25 ml/1 fl oz) 1 unit
Standard glass of wine (175 ml/6 fl oz) 2.1 units
Bottle of beer or cider (330 ml/11 fl oz) 1.7 units

Mood boosters

Leaving home for the first time is a major life event and while it signals a huge leap in your independence, it can also have a big impact on your emotional state. It's normal to feel homesick and, as previously mentioned, it's important to take care of yourself by eating well, exercising and not overindulging on the alcohol front. As you settle into your new life you'll also be putting a lot of pressure on your brain, which makes it even more important to boost your body with bundles of vitamin-rich foods. If you're having a bad day, feeling tired and finding it difficult to concentrate, there are a few foods that can help lift you up and give you a boost. Here are five to get you started:

Water: We should drink about 1.5–2 litres (2¾–3½ pints) of fluid a day and the more of that amount that's made up of water, the better. A small drop in the amount of fluid you drink can very quickly affect your mood and you'll begin to get dehydrated, have a headache and feel tired.

Dark chocolate: Yes, it does contain sugar, but dark chocolate also releases endorphins (happy chemicals) in your brain. Of course, everything in moderation so stick to a couple of squares – just enough to put a smile on your face.

Oily fish: Salmon, sardines, mackerel and tuna all contain omega-3, which is an important nutrient that can help enhance your mood by calming you down if you feel stressed. Plant-based sources of omega-3 include chia seeds, flaxseeds and walnuts.

Green tea: This should be your hot beverage of choice when you're revising for exams – the thiamine in green tea can help you concentrate.

Carbohydrates: These are a vital part of a balanced diet and if you cut out the carbs you might not feel on top form. Carbs help your brain to produce serotonin and a regular in-take of slow-release, wholegrain carbohydrates will help to keep you focused and full of energy.

Hygiene Matters

Use common sense and follow these simple guidelines to avoid food poisoning or the kitchen attracting flies or, even worse, rodents:

Keep it clean: Make sure that the kitchen counters and floor and the fridge – all ideal breeding grounds for bacteria – are cleaned regularly and that the rubbish bin is emptied often. And don't forget about washing tea towels and cleaning cloths, as germs love these too.

Wash your hands: Make sure you wash your hands thoroughly before you start cooking.

Wash fruit and veg: Just think about all the people who will have handled these before they get to you and make sure you wash them.

Defrost meat in the fridge, rather than leaving it out on the kitchen counter.

Pack away chilled and frozen food in the fridge or freezer as soon as you get home.

Keep raw meat covered and on the lowest shelf of the fridge, away from other food to prevent contamination.

Use airtight plastic containers or clingfilm for storing leftovers.

If something looks or smells bad, don't eat it!

breakfast

Banana French Toast

£ · Vegan · <20

SERVES 2

1 ripe banana, plus a few extra banana slices, to serve
200 ml (7 fl oz) dairy-free milk
¼ teaspoon ground cinnamon
4 thick slices of Cheat's Sourdough (see page 199)
2 tablespoons coconut oil or vegan spread
maple syrup, to serve

Mash the banana in a wide, shallow bowl with the back of a fork until smooth. Stir in the dairy-free milk and cinnamon.

Dip the sourdough slices in the banana milk and leave to soak while you preheat a large frying pan over a medium-high heat.

Melt 1 tablespoon of the coconut oil or spread in the pan. Pick 2 slices of bread out of the banana milk and allow the excess to drip off, then add to the pan. Cook for 2 minutes on each side until golden and puffy, then transfer to a plate. Repeat with the remaining bread.

Serve with maple syrup and more banana slices.

TIP
French toast is best made with stale sourdough. If the bread is really dry, splash it with a few drops of water before cooking.

Mustard & Avocado Toast

££ · Vegan · <20

SERVES 1

1 tablespoon Dijon mustard
1 tablespoon vegan mayonnaise
2 thick slices of Cheat's Sourdough (see page 199)
1 avocado, peeled and pitted
1 teaspoon lemon juice
extra virgin olive oil, for drizzling
salt and pepper

Mix the mustard and mayonnaise together in a small bowl, toast the bread, then spread the mustard mixture over the toast.

Put one half of the avocado on each slice of toast, mash with the back of a fork and drizzle with a tiny bit of lemon juice.

Season with salt and pepper and drizzle generously with olive oil before serving.

Porridge

SERVES 2

50 g (2 oz) rolled oats or porridge oats
450 ml (¾ pint) water
pinch of salt
maple syrup or golden syrup, to serve

Put the oats and measured water into a high-sided saucepan and set over a medium heat. Add the salt and bring to the boil. Once boiling, reduce the heat to a bare simmer and cook for 10–15 minutes, stirring occasionally, until the oats are tender and cooked through. The porridge should be thick, but still oozy.

Serve warm with golden syrup or maple syrup. Or you can simply sprinkle with sugar.

TIP

This is perhaps the ultimate broke breakfast. Making porridge with water instead of milk is just as delicious and prevents any scorching or sticking to the base of the pan. Just remember that by volume you need to use a 1:3 ratio – 1 cupful of oats to 3 of water. Feel free to add a splash of milk at the end of cooking to loosen the porridge, if you like. It is wonderful eaten just as it is, but try adding 1 tablespoon of cocoa powder for chocolate porridge, or serving it with jam or fruit compote, or topping with fresh fruit.

Granola

SERVES 10

75 g (3 oz) butter
5 tablespoons honey
1 teaspoon vanilla extract
300 g (10 oz) rolled oats
50 g (2 oz) dried shredded coconut
50 g (2 oz) flaked almonds
3 tablespoons sunflower seeds
3 tablespoons pumpkin seeds
1 tablespoon sesame seeds
1 tablespoon linseeds
75 g (3 oz) rye flakes
75 g (3 oz) ready-to-eat mixed dried fruit, roughly chopped

Put the butter, honey and vanilla extract in a saucepan and cook over a medium heat, stirring occasionally, for 5 minutes or until the honey and butter are combined.

Put the rest of the ingredients, except the fruit, in a large bowl and mix well. Carefully stir in the butter mixture.

Spread the mixture over the base of a large, nonstick tin and bake in a preheated oven, 160°C (325°F), Gas Mark 3, for 20 minutes or until the grains are crisp and browned. Stir occasionally so it doesn't stick.

Take out of the oven and leave to cool, then carefully stir in the dried fruit.

Maple-Glazed Granola with Fruit

SERVES 6

2 tablespoons olive oil
2 tablespoons maple syrup
40 g (1½ oz) flaked almonds
40 g (1½ oz) pine nuts
25 g (1 oz) sunflower seeds
25 g (1 oz) porridge oats
375 ml (13 fl oz) natural yogurt

FRUIT SALAD

1 ripe mango, peeled, pitted and sliced
2 kiwifruit, peeled and sliced
small bunch of red seedless grapes, halved
finely grated zest and juice of 1 lime

Heat the oil in an ovenproof frying pan, then add the maple syrup, nuts, seeds and oats and toss together.

Transfer the pan to a preheated oven, 180°C (350°F), Gas Mark 4, and cook for 5–8 minutes, stirring once and moving the brown edges to the centre, until the granola mixture is evenly toasted.

Leave the mixture to cool, then pack it into a storage jar, seal, label and consume within 10 days.

Make the fruit salad. Mix the fruits with the lime zest and juice, spoon the mixture into bowls and top with spoonfuls of natural yogurt and granola.

Berry, Honey & Yogurt Pots

SERVES 4

400 g (13 oz) frozen mixed berries, defrosted
juice of 1 orange
6 tablespoons honey
400 ml (14 fl oz) vanilla yogurt
50 g (2 oz) granola (see opposite for homemade)

Whizz half of the berries with the orange juice and honey in a blender or food processor until fairly smooth. Transfer to a bowl and stir in the remaining berries.

Divide one-third of the berry mixture between 4 glasses or small bowls. Top with half of the yogurt.

Layer with half of the remaining berry mixture and top with the remaining yogurt.

Top with the remaining berry mixture, then sprinkle over the granola just before serving.

Pumpkin Seed & Apricot Muesli

SERVES 2

50 g (2 oz) jumbo rolled oats
1 tablespoon sultanas or raisins
1 tablespoon pumpkin seeds
1 tablespoon chopped almonds
2 tablespoons chopped ready-to-eat dried apricots
2 tablespoons fruit juice, such as apple or orange juice, or water
2 small apples, peeled and grated
3 tablespoons milk or natural yogurt, to serve

Place the oats, sultanas or raisins, pumpkin seeds, almonds and apricots in a bowl with the fruit juice or water. Add the apple and mix well. Spoon into bowls and serve topped with milk or yogurt.

Bircher Muesli

SERVES 4

200 g (7 oz) buckwheat flakes
300 ml (½ pint) milk
100 ml (3½ fl oz) apple juice
1 apple, peeled and grated

TO SERVE

2 tablespoons honey
100 g (3½ oz) ready-to-eat dried fruit, such as mango, apricots or sultanas
100 g (3½ oz) hazelnuts, toasted and roughly chopped
poached or canned fruit, such as peaches or berries

Mix together the buckwheat flakes, milk, apple juice and apple in a bowl. Cover with clingfilm and leave to soak overnight.

To serve, stir the honey, dried fruit and nuts into the muesli mixture. Spoon into bowls, then top with the poached or canned fruit.

TIP
When it comes to shopping for everyday items, a quick and easy way to save money is to switch from big brands to own brands. Breakfast cereals, condiments, drinks and cleaning products are just some of the own-brand shopping-trolley staples that will slash your budget.

Blueberry Pancakes

£ · Veggie · >20

SERVES 4

125 g (4 oz) self-raising flour
½ teaspoon baking powder
1 tablespoon icing sugar
1 egg
150 ml (¼ pint) milk
125 g (4 oz) blueberries
1 tablespoon vegetable oil
1 tablespoon maple syrup
Greek yogurt and extra blueberries,
   to serve (optional)

In a large bowl mix the flour, baking powder and icing sugar. Add the egg and gradually whisk in the milk to make a smooth batter, then stir in the blueberries.

Heat a little oil in a large frying pan. Pour large spoonfuls of the batter, spaced well apart, into the pan and cook for 2 minutes or until bubbles begin to appear on the surface of the pancakes.

Turn the pancakes over and cook the other side until golden, then take out of the pan. Continue making pancakes until all the batter is used up.

Pile the pancakes onto plates and drizzle with maple syrup. Top each pile with a dollop of Greek yogurt and a few extra blueberries, if liked.

Boiled Egg with Toast

£   Veggie   <20

SERVES 2
4 eggs
25 g (1 oz) butter
salt and pepper
buttered toast, to serve

Boil a saucepan of water then carefully add the eggs to the pan, using a spoon so they do not crack. Boil for 4–5 minutes – the whites should be set but the yolks still runny (boil for an extra couple of minutes if you want the yolks to be set as well).

Remove the eggs from the pan with the spoon and crack open. Sprinkle with salt and pepper and eat with buttered toast.

Vegan Egg Dip

£   Vegan   <20

SERVES 2
235 ml (7½ fl oz) water
1 tablespoon cornflour
3 tablespoons nutritional yeast
½ teaspoon ground turmeric
salt and pepper

Put all the ingredients for the dip into a small saucepan. Bring to the boil over a medium heat, whisking constantly, until thickened and glossy. Season to taste.

Serve the sauce in egg cups or small bowls, with soldiers to dip in.

TIP
This salty, savoury vibrant yellow sauce is reminiscent of a dippy (soft-boiled) egg. It contains only a handful of ingredients and is super simple to make.

EGGS

Fried Eggs

SERVES 2

1 tablespoon vegetable oil
2 eggs

TIP

Simply eat with toast or serve with grilled tomatoes, mushrooms and fried bread for a full breakfast. If you prefer your yolks better cooked, flip the eggs over just before you take them out of the pan.

Heat the oil in a frying pan until it is really hot but not smoking or burning.

Break an egg into a cup, remove any shell, then tip into the frying pan. The white should begin to set immediately. Repeat with the second egg.

Turn the heat down to medium and spoon the oil over the eggs so the tops cook as well. Cook for about a minute until the whites are set but the yolks are still runny. Use a fish slice or spatula to remove the eggs from the pan so that the yolks don't break

Poached Eggs

SERVES 1

1 tablespoon vinegar
2 eggs
buttered toast, to serve

Pour about 4 cm (1½ inches) of water into a saucepan or frying pan and add the vinegar (this helps the white to stick to the yolk). Bring the water to the boil, then turn down the heat so it is just simmering (not boiling violently).

Break an egg into a cup and slide it carefully into the water. If you need to, gently stir the water around the egg so that the white makes a neat round shape. Repeat with the other egg.

Poach for 3–5 minutes over a very low heat, until the whites are set but the yolks are still runny. Take the poached eggs out of the pan with a spoon and eat straight away with buttered toast.

Scrambled Eggs

£ | Veggie | <20

SERVES 1
2 eggs
1 tablespoon milk
15 g (½ oz) butter
salt and pepper
buttered toast, to serve

Crack the eggs into a bowl and beat with a fork, adding the milk and a sprinkling of salt and pepper.

Melt the butter in a saucepan (ideally use a nonstick saucepan because scrambled egg tends to stick) over a low heat, then add the egg mixture. Stir the eggs with a wooden spoon until the eggs have scrambled and have just set, then take off the heat and eat straight away with buttered toast.

TIP
If you want to jazz up simple scrambled eggs, try adding some fresh chopped herbs or grated cheese, and serve with warm croissants or slices of ciabatta. A real treat.

Banana & Sultana Drop Scones

£ Veggie

SERVES 10

125 g (4 oz) self-raising flour
2 tablespoons caster sugar
½ teaspoon baking powder
1 small ripe banana, peeled and roughly mashed
1 egg, beaten
150 ml (¼ pint) milk
50 g (2 oz) sultanas
vegetable oil, for greasing
butter, honey, or golden or maple syrup, to serve

TIP

For summer berry drop scones, prepare the recipe as above, but stir in 125 g (4 oz) mixed fresh blueberries and raspberries instead of the sultanas.

Put the flour, sugar and baking powder in a mixing bowl. Add the mashed banana with the egg. Gradually whisk in the milk with a fork until the mixture resembles a smooth thick batter. Stir in the sultanas.

Pour a little oil on to a piece of folded kitchen paper and use to grease a griddle or heavy-based nonstick frying pan. Heat the pan, then drop heaped dessert spoonfuls of the mixture (in batches), well spaced apart, on to the pan. Cook for 2 minutes until bubbles appear on the top and the undersides are golden. Turn over and cook for a further 1–2 minutes until the second side is done.

Serve warm, topped with 1 teaspoon butter, honey, or golden or maple syrup per scone. These are best eaten on the day they are made.

Seeded Spelt Soda Bread

£ Veggie

SERVES 8

vegetable oil, for greasing
250 g (8 oz) spelt flour, plus extra for dusting
100 g (3½ oz) rye flour
2 teaspoons baking powder
1 teaspoon salt
40 g (1½ oz) pumpkin seeds
40 g (1½ oz) sunflower seeds
284 ml (9½ fl oz) carton buttermilk
100 ml (3½ fl oz) semi-skimmed milk

TIP

Breadcrumbs. When you get to the last slice of bread, don't throw it away if it's a bit dry – blitz it in a blender and keep the breadcrumbs in an airtight container in the freezer. They're great for pie and bake toppings.

Grease a loaf tin with a capacity of at least 750 ml (1¼ pints). If you don't have a loaf tin, grease a baking sheet.

Sift the flours and baking powder into a bowl. Tip in the grain left in the sieve and stir in the salt and seeds. Add the buttermilk and milk and mix with a round-bladed knife to form a soft dough.

Turn out on to a lightly floured surface and shape into an oblong. Turn into the prepared tin or neaten the shape and place on the baking sheet. Bake in a preheated oven, 200°C (400°F), Gas Mark 6, for 20 minutes.

Reduce the oven temperature to 160°C (325°F), Gas Mark 3, and bake for a further 15 minutes. Turn out of the tin (if using) and return to the oven shelf for a further 10 minutes baking. Leave to cool completely on a wire rack. Serve in slices. This is best eaten on the day it is made.

Frozen Fruit Smoothie Bowl

£ · Vegan · <20

SERVES 2

2 frozen bananas (see tip)
400 g (13 oz) frozen berries, plus extra to serve
2 tablespoons unsweetened desiccated coconut

Put all the frozen fruit in a blender and blitz until smooth and thick.

Pour the smoothie into 2 bowls. Serve topped with extra frozen berries and sprinkled with coconut.

TIP

Buying pre-packaged frozen fruit works out a lot cheaper than the fresh stuff. You can also freeze your own berries and bananas when they're looking a little past their best, then throw them straight into a blender for a quick, thick morning smoothie bowl. To freeze bananas, peel them, then slice them or leave them whole. Lay them – well spaced apart – on a baking tray until frozen solid, then transfer to a freezerproof container or bag. Freeze berries in the same way, to stop them clumping together.

DRINKS

Breakfast Smoothie

£ · Veggie · <20

SERVES 2–3

1 tablespoon pomegranate juice
1 small ripe banana, peeled and sliced
300 ml (½ pint) soya milk
1 tablespoon almonds
1 tablespoon rolled oats
½ teaspoon honey
1½ teaspoons ground linseeds
2 tablespoons natural yogurt

Place all the ingredients in a blender or food processor and blend until smooth and creamy.

Pour into 2-3 glasses and serve immediately.

TIP
Wise up to water. It really is the elixir of life so try to make sure you drink more aqua than alcohol. Keep a bottle in your bag and drink regularly throughout the day to keep your brain alert and lethargy at bay.

£   Veggie

Banana & Peanut Butter Smoothie

>50

SERVES 2

1 ripe banana
300 ml (½ pint) semi-skimmed milk
1 tablespoon smooth peanut butter or
   2 teaspoons tahini

Peel and slice the banana, put it in a freezerproof container and freeze for at least 2 hours or overnight.

Put the frozen banana, the milk and peanut butter or tahini in a blender or food processor and blend until smooth.

Pour into 2 glasses and serve immediately.

TIP

Tahini is a delicious paste made from crushed sesame seeds. Weight for weight, sesame seeds contain ten times more calcium than milk. This smoothie is an excellent source of vitamins C, B1, B2, B6 and B12, folic acid, niacin, calcium, copper, potassium, zinc, magnesium and phosphorus.

££   Veggie

Avocado & Banana Smoothie

<20

SERVES 1

1 small ripe avocado
1 small ripe banana
250 ml (8 fl oz) skimmed milk
ice cubes, to serve

Peel the avocado, remove the stone and roughly chop the flesh. Peel and slice the banana.

Place the avocado, banana and milk in a blender or food processor and blend together until smooth.

Pour into a glass, add a couple of ice cubes and serve immediately.

TIP

In the tropics, avocados are often called poor man's butter because of their creamy texture and high fat content. Unlike butter, though, most of the fat is monounsaturated – the sort that helps lower levels of the 'bad' cholesterol (or low-density lipoproteins) while raising levels of the 'good' cholesterol (or high-density lipoproteins). Just one avocado provides around half the recommended daily intake of vitamin B6. This smoothie is an excellent source of vitamins C, E, B1, B2, B6 and B12, as well as folic acid, calcium, potassium, copper, zinc, magnesium and phosphorus.

Gingered Apple & Carrot Juice

SERVES 2

375 g (12 oz) carrots, peeled and cut into chunks
3 dessert apples, cored and cut into chunks
2.5 cm (1 inch) piece of fresh root ginger, peeled

Feed the carrot and apple chunks through a juicer with the ginger.

Pour the juice into 2 glasses and serve immediately.

Cardamom Coffee

SERVES 4

3 tablespoons strong, freshly ground coffee (South Indian, Colombian or Javan)
1 teaspoon crushed cardamom seeds
250 ml (8 fl oz) milk
2 tablespoons sugar
600 ml (1 pint) water

Place the coffee, cardamom seeds, milk, sugar and measured water in a large saucepan and bring to the boil. Reduce the heat and simmer for 1–2 minutes.

Using a very fine-meshed sieve lined with muslin, strain the coffee into mugs and serve hot.

Lemon Grass Tea

SERVES 4

3–4 lemon grass stalks, finely chopped
4 teaspoons Indian tea leaves (Darjeeling or Assam)
750 ml (1¼ pints) water
milk and sugar, to serve (optional)

Put the lemon grass and tea leaves in a large saucepan with the measured water and bring to the boil. Reduce the heat and simmer, uncovered, for 2–3 minutes.

Using a very fine-meshed sieve lined with muslin, strain the tea into mugs and serve hot, adding milk and sugar to taste.

brunch

Hash Browns

£ | Vegan | >50

MAKES 8

500 g (1 lb) floury potatoes, peeled
50 g (2 oz) cornflour, plus extra if needed
flavourless oil, for frying
salt and pepper
tomato ketchup, to serve

Use the coarse side of a grater to grate the potatoes into a bowl of very cold water, then leave for 30 minutes, or up to 2 hours, to allow the potatoes to release any starch.

Drain and rinse the grated potato, then bring a saucepan of water to the boil. Drop in the grated potato and blanch for 3–4 minutes – this helps the hash browns to be extra fluffy inside.

Drain and rinse the potato again under cold water, then place in a clean tea towel. Wring out the majority of the liquid – this will allow the hash browns to get crispy edges. You still want a little moisture clinging to the potato strands though, to allow you to shape them.

Tip the potato into a bowl, stir in the cornflour and season well with salt and pepper. The mixture may look dry at first but, when you shape them, the potato will release more moisture.

Shape into 8 hash browns using your hands, sprinkling over more cornflour if the mix is too wet and won't hold together.

Heat enough oil for frying in a deep-sided frying pan, about 2.5 cm (1 inch) deep, over a medium heat. Carefully fry the hash browns for 5–6 minutes on each side until golden. Serve immediately with an extra sprinkling of salt and some tomato ketchup.

TIP
These perfect hash browns only use three ingredients: potatoes, cornflour and oil. You can add 1 teaspoon of onion powder to get that traditional fast food flavour if you like, but they're also delicious without. The method does take a little while, but the results are worth it.

£ Veggie

Omelette with Cherry Tomatoes

<20

SERVES 4

3 tablespoons olive oil
125 g (4 oz) cherry tomatoes
2 tablespoons chopped mixed herbs (such as
  basil, chives, mint, tarragon or thyme)
1 teaspoon grated lemon zest
3 eggs
1 tablespoon red pesto
2 tablespoons milk
salt and pepper
green salad, to serve (optional)

Heat 2 tablespoons of the oil in a frying pan and fry the tomatoes, herbs and lemon zest for 3 minutes until the tomatoes start to soften. Take off the heat and keep warm.

Crack the eggs into a bowl and beat well. Add the pesto, milk and a dash of salt and pepper and beat again.

Melt the rest of the oil in a frying pan over a medium heat, then tip in the eggs.

Leave for a few seconds then, using a fork or spoon, scrape the mixture away from the edge of the pan into the centre, so the mixture runs to the sides. Do this a couple of times until the mixture is set, which should take 3–4 minutes.

Spoon on the tomato mixture, flip over the omelette, cook for another minute, then eat straight away with a green salad, if liked.

Chorizo & Ham Eggs

SERVES 2

1 tablespoon olive oil
1 small red pepper, cored, deseeded and sliced
125 g (4 oz) chorizo sausage, thinly sliced
2 tomatoes, roughly chopped
50 g (2 oz) wafer-thin ham slices
2 handfuls of baby spinach leaves
2 large eggs
warm crusty bread, to serve

Heat the oil in a frying pan, add the red pepper and chorizo and cook over a high heat for 2 minutes until golden. Add the tomatoes and cook for a further 2 minutes, then add the ham and spinach and cook, stirring occasionally, for 2 minutes.

Divide the mixture between 2 small, individual pans, if you have them (if not, continue to cook in one pan). Make wells in the tomato mixture and break an egg into each well. Cover and cook for 2–3 minutes over a medium heat until set. Serve with warm crusty bread to mop up the juices.

Huevos Rancheros

SERVES 4

2 tablespoons olive oil
1 large onion, diced
2 red peppers, cored, deseeded and diced
2 garlic cloves, crushed
¾ teaspoon dried oregano
400 g (13 oz) can chopped tomatoes
4 eggs
20 g (¾ oz) feta cheese, crumbled
4 toasted pitta breads, to serve

Heat the oil in a frying pan over a medium heat, then add the onion, peppers, garlic and oregano and cook for 5 minutes.

Add the tomatoes and cook for a further 5 minutes. Pour the tomato mixture into a shallow ovenproof dish and make 4 dips in the mixture.

Crack the eggs into the dips, sprinkle with the feta and cook under a preheated hot grill for 3–4 minutes. Serve with toasted pitta breads.

TIP

Eggs – cheap and nutritious student staples – get a Mexican makeover in this dish. Traditionally served for breakfast, it makes a great meal any time.

Haddock with Poached Eggs

SERVES 4

750 g (1½ lb) new potatoes
4 spring onions, sliced
2 tablespoons half-fat crème fraîche
75 g (3 oz) watercress
4 smoked haddock fillets, about 150 g (5 oz) each
150 ml (¼ pint) milk
1 bay leaf
4 eggs
pepper

Place the potatoes in a saucepan of boiling water and cook for 12–15 minutes until tender. Drain, lightly crush with a fork, then stir through the spring onions, crème fraîche and watercress and season well with pepper. Keep warm.

Put the fish and milk in a large frying pan with the bay leaf. Bring to the boil, then cover and simmer for 5–6 minutes until the fish is cooked through. Remove from the heat and let stand while you poach the eggs.

Bring a saucepan of water to the boil, swirl the water with a spoon and crack in an egg, allowing the white to wrap around the yolk. Simmer for 3 minutes, then remove and keep warm. Repeat with the remaining eggs.

Serve the drained poached haddock on top of the crushed potatoes, topped with the poached eggs.

Smoked Mackerel Kedgeree

SERVES 4

3 large eggs
25 g (1 oz) butter
375 g (12 oz) smoked mackerel, skinned and flaked
375 g (12 oz) cooked basmati rice
1 teaspoon mild curry powder
4 tablespoons lemon juice
4 tablespoons chopped parsley

Place the eggs in a small saucepan of boiling water and cook them for 7 minutes. Drain, run under cold water, then shell them and cut into quarters.

Meanwhile, melt the butter in a frying pan, add the smoked mackerel, rice and curry powder and toss together until everything is warmed through and the rice is evenly coated.

Stir in the lemon juice, parsley and the quartered boiled eggs and serve immediately.

TIP
Bag a bargain. If you have space in your freezer, make the most of supermarket bargains and tuck them away for when the budget is straining.

Egg Pots with Smoked Salmon

SERVES 4

butter, for greasing
200 g (7 oz) smoked salmon trimmings
2 tablespoons chopped chives
4 eggs
4 tablespoons double cream
pepper
buttered bread, to serve

Grease 4 ramekins with butter. Divide the smoked salmon and chives among the prepared ramekins. Using the back of a spoon, make a small hollow in the top of the salmon in each ramekin. Break an egg into each hollow, sprinkle with a little pepper and spoon the cream over the top.

Put the ramekins in a roasting tin and half-fill the tin with boiling water. Bake in a preheated oven, 180°C (350°F), Gas Mark 4, for 10–15 minutes until the eggs have just set.

Remove from the oven and leave to cool for a few minutes, then serve with the buttered bread.

Chilli Garlic Mushrooms

SERVES 2

3 tablespoons olive oil
300 g (10 oz) chestnut mushrooms, finely sliced
2 garlic cloves, finely sliced
1 red chilli, deseeded and finely chopped
leaves from 3 thyme sprigs
salt and pepper

Preheat a large frying pan over a medium-high heat and add the olive oil. Fry the mushrooms for 3–4 minutes on each side until deeply golden.

Once you are happy that your mushrooms have enough colour, add the garlic, chilli and thyme and cook for 1 minute until fragrant.

Season well with salt and pepper, then serve with toast, if you like, or as part of a full cooked breakfast.

TIP

The trick to cooking really delicious mushrooms is to fry them either in batches or in a big enough pan so that they can turn really golden and caramelized. It is nearly impossible to burn a mushroom, so don't be afraid to get the pan nice and hot – the rest of the flavourings are added after the mushrooms are fully cooked to prevent that bitter, burned garlic taste. Feel free to omit the chilli here or swap the thyme for parsley. Mushrooms are great vehicles for flavour, so use whatever you have to hand.

Baked Mushrooms with Goats' Cheese & Rocket

£ Veggie >20

SERVES 4

500 g (1 lb) new potatoes, halved
3 tablespoons olive oil
200 g (7 oz) portobello mushrooms
2 tablespoons chopped thyme
6 garlic cloves, unpeeled
50 g (2 oz) soft goats' cheese
125 g (4 oz) cherry tomatoes
salt and pepper
25 g (1 oz) toasted pine nuts, to garnish
75 g (3 oz) rocket, to serve

Put the potatoes in a large roasting tin, drizzle over 2 tablespoons of the olive oil and toss to make sure the potatoes are well coated in oil. Bake in a preheated oven, 220°C (425°F), Gas Mark 7, for 15 minutes, turning once halfway through the cooking time.

Add the mushrooms, stem-side up, to the tin, scatter over the thyme and garlic, drizzle over the remaining oil and season well with salt and pepper. Place a little goats' cheese on top of each mushroom and return to the oven for a further 5 minutes.

Add the cherry tomatoes to the tin and return to the oven for 5 minutes more, or until the potatoes and mushrooms are cooked through. Garnish with the pine nuts and serve with the rocket.

Tarragon Mushroom Toasts

££ Veggie <20

SERVES 4

8 slices of brioche
150 g (5 oz) butter
2 banana shallots, finely chopped
3 garlic cloves, finely chopped
1 red chilli, deseeded and finely chopped
  (optional)
300 g (10 oz) mixed wild mushrooms, such as
  chanterelle, cep, girolle and oyster, or white
  mushrooms, trimmed and sliced
4 tablespoons crème fraîche, plus extra to garnish
  (optional)
2 tablespoons finely chopped tarragon
1 tablespoon finely chopped parsley
salt and pepper

Toast the brioche slices lightly and keep warm.

Heat the butter in a frying pan and fry the shallots, garlic and chilli, if using, for 1–2 minutes. Add the mushrooms and stir-fry over a medium heat for 6–8 minutes. Season well with salt and pepper, then remove from the heat and stir in the crème fraîche and herbs.

Spoon the mushrooms on to the toasted brioche and serve immediately, with an extra dollop of crème fraîche, if liked.

Whole-Can Tangy Black Beans

SERVES 6

2 tablespoons olive oil
1 onion, finely chopped
3 garlic cloves, finely chopped
2 x 400 g (13 oz) cans black beans
400 ml (14 fl oz) water or vegan stock
½ teaspoon ground cumin
½ teaspoon ground coriander
½ teaspoon smoked paprika
1 tablespoon caster sugar
1 tablespoon apple cider vinegar
salt and pepper

Heat the oil in a large frying pan. Add the onion and garlic and cook for 6–8 minutes over a medium heat until softened.

Add the beans and their liquid to the pan, then add the water or stock to the cans and swirl to make sure you loosen every last drop before adding that too.

Season with the spices, sugar and salt and pepper. Stir well and cook for 15 minutes over a medium heat, stirring occasionally, until thickened. Use a spoon to smash some of the beans, to help to thicken the mixture, or use a hand blender to blitz half the beans roughly.

Take the pan off the heat, stir in the vinegar and season to taste. The beans will thicken further as they cool.

Eat immediately, or store in the refrigerator in an airtight container for up to 5 days. This freezes well; just make sure it's fully cooled before freezing.

Tomato & Basil Tart

SERVES 4

butter for greasing
375 g (12 oz) ready-made puff pastry
plain flour, for dusting
1 egg, beaten
200 g (7 oz) mascarpone cheese
50 g (2 oz) Parmesan cheese, grated
handful of chopped basil, plus extra to garnish
150 g (5 oz) cherry tomatoes, halved
1 tablespoon olive oil
salt and pepper

Lightly grease a baking sheet with butter. On a clean surface, lightly dusted with plain flour, roll out the pastry to a 30 cm (12 inch) disc. Place on the prepared baking sheet and roll the edges up to create a 1 cm (½ inch) border. Press the border down with your thumb to make a crumpled edge, then prick over the middle of the pastry disc a few times with a fork. Place in the freezer for a few minutes.

Brush the border of the pastry with a little of the beaten egg. Mix together the mascarpone, remaining egg, Parmesan and basil in a bowl, season to taste with salt and pepper and spread over the centre of the tart. Arrange the tomatoes on top of the tart and drizzle over the oil. Bake in a preheated oven, 220°C (425°F), Gas Mark 7, for 20–25 minutes until golden and crisp.

Smashed Chickpeas with Tomatoes

SERVES 2

400 g (13 oz) can chickpeas, drained and rinsed
4 tablespoons tahini
2 tablespoons olive oil, plus extra for drizzling
large handful of flat leaf parsley, finely chopped,
  plus extra to serve
4 thick slices of Cheat's Sourdough (see page 199)
10 cherry tomatoes, halved
salt and pepper

TO SERVE

lemon wedges
1 teaspoon paprika

Put the chickpeas in a bowl and use a potato masher to crush them, then add the tahini and olive oil and continue to crush until you reach your desired consistency. Some brands of canned chickpeas may need to be flashed in the microwave for 10–20 seconds to soften, if they prove too hard to mash.

Season with salt and pepper and fold in the parsley. Toast the bread.

Heap the chickpea mixture on the toast and top with the tomatoes. Serve with lemon wedges, a sprinkling of paprika and parsley.

TIP

If the only things you smash are avocados, you're going to rack up quite a hefty bill. Chickpeas are affordable and are amazing on toast because they take on whatever flavour you add. Try tossing them with chilli sauce or pesto for another variation.

Feed-a-Cold Chicken Soup

££ >20

SERVES 4

1.2 litres (2 pints) hot chicken or vegetable stock (see page 197)
1 bay leaf
500 g (1 lb) boneless, skinless chicken thighs, trimmed of fat
25 g (1 oz) butter
1 celery stick, thinly sliced
2 leeks, trimmed, cleaned and thinly sliced
2 carrots, thinly sliced
125 g (4 oz) mushrooms, sliced
1 garlic clove, chopped
75 g (3 oz) frozen sweetcorn
75 g (3 oz) angel hair pasta
salt and pepper
chilli oil, to drizzle (optional)
chopped parsley, to garnish

Bring the stock and bay leaf to the boil in a saucepan and add the chicken. Cover loosely and simmer for 20 minutes, until cooked and tender. Scoop out the meat with a slotted spoon and set aside to cool slightly, reserving the stock.

Meanwhile, melt the butter in a large pan and cook the celery, leeks and carrots for 7–8 minutes, until softened. Add the mushrooms and garlic and cook for further 3–4 minutes.

Pour in the reserved stock, add the corn and return to the boil. Season to taste. Tip the pasta into the pan and cook for 3–4 minutes, or until al dente.

Shred the chicken and add to the broth. Ladle into bowls and serve drizzled with chilli oil, if liked, and garnished with chopped parsley and freshly ground pepper.

soups

Spicy Coriander & Lentil Soup

£

>50

SERVES 8

500 g (1 lb) red lentils
2 tablespoons vegetable oil
2 onions, chopped
2 garlic cloves, chopped
2 celery sticks, chopped
400 g (13 oz) can tomatoes
1 chilli, deseeded and chopped (optional)
1 teaspoon paprika
1 teaspoon harissa paste
1 teaspoon ground cumin
1.2 litres (2 pints) vegetable stock (see page 197)
  salt and pepper
2 tablespoons chopped coriander, to garnish

Place the lentils in a bowl of water. Heat the oil in a large saucepan and gently fry the onions, garlic and celery over a low heat until softened.

Drain the lentils and add them to the vegetable pan with the tomatoes, mixing well. Add the chilli, if using, paprika, harissa paste, cumin and vegetable stock and season with salt and pepper. Cover the pan and simmer gently for about 40–50 minutes until the lentils are tender, adding a little more vegetable stock or water if the soup gets too thick.

Serve the soup immediately in warmed individual bowls topped with a little chopped coriander.

Hearty Minestrone

£   Veggie

>20

SERVES 4

3 carrots, roughly chopped
1 red onion, roughly chopped
6 celery sticks, roughly chopped
2 tablespoons olive oil
2 garlic cloves, crushed
200 g (7 oz) potatoes, peeled and cut into
  1 cm (½ inch) dice
4 tablespoons tomato purée
1.5 litres (2½ pints) vegetable stock (see page 197)
400 g (13 oz) can chopped tomatoes
150 g (5 oz) short-shaped soup pasta
400 g (13 oz) can cannellini beans, rinsed
  and drained
100 g (3½ oz) spinach leaves
salt and pepper
crusty bread, to serve

Whizz the carrots, onion and celery in a blender or food processor until finely chopped.

Heat the oil in a large saucepan, add the chopped vegetables, garlic, potatoes, tomato purée, stock, tomatoes and pasta. Bring to the boil, then reduce the heat and simmer, covered, for 12–15 minutes, stirring occasionally.

Tip in the cannellini beans and the spinach for the final 2 minutes of the cooking time.

Season to taste with salt and pepper and serve with crusty bread.

Butternut & Rosemary Soup

£ · Vegan · >50

SERVES 4

1 butternut squash, halved, deseeded and cut into small chunks
few rosemary sprigs, plus extra leaves to garnish
150 g (5 oz) red lentils, rinsed and drained
1 onion, finely chopped
900 ml (1½ pints) vegetable stock (see page 197)
salt and pepper

Place the squash pieces in a nonstick roasting tin. Sprinkle over the rosemary sprigs and season with salt and pepper. Roast in a preheated oven, 200°C (400°F), Gas Mark 6, for 45 minutes.

Meanwhile, put the lentils in a saucepan and cover with water, then bring to the boil and boil rapidly for 10 minutes. Drain, then return to a clean saucepan with the onion and stock and simmer for 5 minutes. Season with salt and pepper.

Remove the squash from the oven and scoop the flesh from the skin. Next, mash the flesh with a fork and add it to the soup, then simmer for 25 minutes, stirring occasionally, until the lentils are tender. Serve the soup scattered with extra rosemary.

Sweet Potato & Cabbage Soup

£ · >20

SERVES 4

2 onions, chopped
2 garlic cloves, sliced
4 lean back bacon rashers, chopped
500 g (1 lb) sweet potatoes, scrubbed or peeled and chopped
2 parsnips, chopped
1 teaspoon chopped thyme
900 ml (1½ pints) vegetable stock (see page 197)
1 baby Savoy cabbage, shredded
Seeded Spelt Soda Bread (see page 25), to serve (optional)

Place the onions, garlic and bacon in a large saucepan and fry for 2–3 minutes. Add the sweet potatoes, parsnips, thyme and stock to the saucepan, then bring to the boil and simmer for 15 minutes, stirring occasionally.

Cool slightly, then transfer two-thirds of the soup to a blender or food processor and blend until smooth. Return to the pan, add the cabbage and simmer for 5–7 minutes until the cabbage is just cooked. Serve with soda bread, if liked.

VARIATION

For **squash and broccoli soup**, follow the recipe above, replacing the sweet potatoes with 500 g (1 lb) peeled, deseeded and chopped butternut squash. After returning the blended soup to the pan, add 100 g (3½ oz) small broccoli florets. Cook as above, omitting the cabbage.

Winter Veg & Beer Broth

£   Veggie   >50

SERVES 6

4 tablespoons olive oil
1 onion, chopped
2 garlic cloves, crushed
1 tablespoon chopped rosemary
2 carrots, diced
250 g (8 oz) parsnips, diced
250 g (8 oz) swede, diced
100 g (3½ oz) pearl barley
600 ml (1 pint) beer or lager
1 litre (1¾ pints) vegetable stock (see page 197)
2 tablespoons chopped parsley
salt and pepper
crusty bread, to serve

Heat the oil in a large saucepan, add the onion, garlic, rosemary, carrots, parsnips and swede and cook over a low heat, stirring frequently, for 10 minutes.

Stir in the barley, beer or lager, stock and salt and pepper and bring to the boil. Reduce the heat, cover and simmer gently for 40–45 minutes until the barley and vegetables are tender.

Stir in the parsley and adjust the seasoning. Serve with plenty of crusty bread.

VARIATION

For **vegetable & rice soup**, omit the beer and increase the stock to 1.5 litres (21/2 pints). Replace the barley with an equal quantity of risotto rice. Use 250 g (8 oz) celeriac instead of the parsnips. Continue the recipe as above.

Easy Tomato Soup

<20

SERVES 4

300 g (10 oz) can condensed tomato soup
400 g (13 oz) can tomatoes, sieved
325 g (11 oz) can sweetcorn, drained
1 tablespoon soy sauce
3–6 drops Tabasco sauce
1 teaspoon chopped oregano
½ teaspoon sugar
125 g (4 oz) Cheddar cheese, grated

Put all the ingredients, except the cheese, in a large saucepan and cook over a medium heat stirring all the time. Bring to the boil, then turn down the heat and simmer, uncovered, for 3 minutes.

Pour the soup into ovenproof bowls, sprinkle with cheese and place under a hot grill for 3–5 minutes until the cheese is bubbling. Delicious served with crusty wholemeal bread.

£ Vegan

Chickpea & Red Pepper Soup

<20

SERVES 4

2 tablespoons olive oil
1 onion, finely chopped
1 red pepper, cored, deseeded and chopped
2 garlic cloves, crushed
2 teaspoons tomato purée
1 teaspoon ground cumin
½ teaspoon ground coriander
pinch of cayenne pepper
pinch of saffron threads
1.5 litres (2½ pints) hot vegetable stock (see page 197)
400 g (13 oz) can chickpeas, rinsed and drained
125 g (4 oz) couscous
finely grated zest and juice of 1 lemon
salt and pepper

TO GARNISH

handful of chopped mint
handful of chopped fresh coriander

Heat the oil in a large heavy-based saucepan. Add the onion and cook for 5 minutes, then add the red pepper, garlic, tomato purée and spices and cook for a further 1 minute.

Pour in the stock and bring to the boil, then reduce the heat and simmer for 5 minutes. Add the chickpeas and simmer for a further 5 minutes, then season to taste with salt and pepper.

Add the couscous and a squeeze of lemon juice and cook for 1 minute, or until the couscous is tender. Ladle into bowls and garnish with the chopped herbs and grated lemon zest.

Foolproof Glorious Gazpacho

£ · Vegan · <20

SERVES 8–10

875 g (1¾ lb) tomatoes, roughly chopped

1 red pepper, cored, deseeded and roughly chopped

1 small red onion, quartered

1 garlic clove

1 cucumber, roughly chopped

1 stale slice of bread (about 125 g/4 oz)

2 tablespoons sherry vinegar or red wine vinegar, or to taste

2 tablespoons caster sugar, or to taste

2 tablespoons extra virgin olive oil or regular olive oil, plus extra for drizzling

salt and pepper

TO SERVE (OPTIONAL)

¼ cucumber, finely chopped

small handful of cherry tomatoes, sliced

small handful of basil leaves

In a large blender, or in a large bowl with a hand blender, blitz all the soup ingredients together, seasoning well with salt and pepper. Taste and add more sugar or vinegar depending on the sweetness of your tomatoes – you're looking for a sharp and sweet soup with a slight spicy burn from the garlic.

You can eat the soup as is, or pass it through a sieve to get a smoother result.

Refrigerate before serving sprinkled with salt and pepper and drizzled with olive oil, or with chopped cucumber, sliced tomatoes and basil leaves.

TIP

This is simply summer in a bowl and, with no cooking required, you can stay cool in the kitchen. Pick up a bargain at your local greengrocer or farmers' market, plumping for those tomatoes that are a bit squished and ugly (it's all getting blitzed together anyway). This silky-smooth soup is best served chilled, so it's good to put it in the refrigerator for at least 1 hour before serving, or pop in a few ice cubes before eating, if you run out of time.

Coconut Noodles in a Mug

£ · Veggie · <20

SERVES 1

3 spring onions, thinly sliced

100 g (3½ oz) courgette, grated

1 teaspoon olive oil

100 ml (3½ fl oz) coconut milk

¼ teaspoon vegetable bouillon powder

½ teaspoon Thai spice powder, such as Thai 7 spice or Thai 5 spice

good pinch of ground turmeric (optional)

75 ml (3 fl oz) boiling water

25 g (1 oz) vermicelli rice noodles

10 cashew nuts, roughly chopped

Mix together the spring onions, courgette and oil in a large, microwave-proof mug and microwave on medium power for 2 minutes.

Stir in the coconut milk, bouillon powder, Thai spice, turmeric, if using, and the boiling water. Microwave on medium power for 1 minute.

Break the noodles into the mug and stir to mix. Microwave on medium power for 1 minute. Stir again and microwave on medium power for a further 1½ minutes until the noodles are tender. Sprinkle with the cashew nuts and serve.

Pimped Instant Ramen

SERVES 2

2 single-portion packets instant ramen noodles
2 tablespoons soy sauce
1 teaspoon chilli oil
1 head of bok choi, halved lengthways
100 g (3½ oz) sweetcorn
1–2 spring onions, finely sliced
1 red chilli, deseeded and finely sliced
small handful of coriander, roughly chopped

£

Vegan

<20

Cook the ramen noodles according to the pack instructions. Add the soy sauce and chilli oil to the broth and leave to cook for another 2 minutes.

Heat a frying pan over a high heat and char the cut sides of the bok choi halves. Add the sweetcorn and allow to fry until charred and caramelized too.

Top the ramen with the charred bok choi and sweetcorn and sprinkle over the spring onions, chilli slices and coriander before serving.

TIP

More instant ramen packets are vegan than you might expect. This is a speedy and simple lunch. Use any vegetables you have in the refrigerator – the ingredients here are just a guide.

Sweet Potato Quesadillas

SERVES 2
2 sweet potatoes (total weight 500–600 g/1 lb 5 oz)
2 tablespoons finely chopped pickled jalapeños
2 spring onions, finely sliced
large handful of coriander, finely chopped
1 lime
2 large tortillas
2 tablespoons flavourless oil
salt and pepper

£

Vegan

<20

Prick the sweet potatoes all over with a knife and microwave on high for 5–7 minutes until tender. Cut in half, then scoop out the flesh into a bowl.

Mix the sweet potato flesh with the jalapeños. Add most of the spring onions and coriander, reserving some of both for serving. Finely grate over the zest of the lime, then cut the lime in half and add the juice of half the lime to season the filling. Cut the other half into wedges for serving.

Distribute the filling between the 2 tortillas, heaping it on half of each tortilla, then folding over the empty side and pressing it down to make sure the filling is in an even layer.

Heat the oil in a large frying pan and add the tortillas. Fry for 2–3 minutes on each side until golden brown and the filling is warm inside.

Cut into wedges and serve with the reserved spring onions and coriander, and the lime wedges.

VARIATION
Try adding **Whole-Can Tangy Black Beans** (see page 39) or other vegetables into the mix. The method of cooking the quesadillas in semi-circles rather than sandwiching the filling between 2 circles ensures you don't lose any filling when flipping them.

Goats' Cheese & Spinach Quesadillas

££ · **Veggie** · **>20**

SERVES 4

275 g (9 oz) baby spinach leaves
8 soft flour tortillas
250 g (8 oz) goats' cheese
2 tablespoons drained, chopped sun-dried tomatoes
2 ripe avocados, peeled, pitted and diced
1 red onion, thinly sliced
juice of 1 lime
2 tablespoons chopped coriander
salt and pepper

Place the spinach in a saucepan with a small amount of water, then cover and cook until wilted. Drain and squeeze dry.

Heat a nonstick frying pan over medium heat until hot, add 1 tortilla and then crumble a quarter of the goats' cheese, followed by a quarter of the spinach and sun-dried tomatoes, over the tortilla. Season lightly with salt and pepper.

Place 1 tortilla on top and cook for 3–4 minutes until golden underneath. Carefully turn the quesadilla over and cook for a further 3–4 minutes. Remove from the pan and keep warm. Repeat with the remaining 6 tortillas.

Meanwhile, mix together the avocados, onion, lime juice and coriander in a bowl.

Serve the warm quesadillas cut into wedges with the avocado salsa.

Chicken Shawarma

£ · **<20**

SERVES 1

1 teaspoon olive or vegetable oil
½ onion, thinly sliced
200 g (7 oz) boneless, skinless chicken thighs, cut into large pieces
1 teaspoon shawarma spice
1 wholemeal pitta bread
1 tablespoon tahini
1 teaspoon honey
1 teaspoon white or red wine vinegar
4 teaspoons hot water
1 Little Gem lettuce
1 gherkin, sliced
salt and pepper

Heat the oil in a small frying pan and fry the onion for 3 minutes until softened. Add the chicken and fry for a further 5 minutes, stirring frequently until the chicken is cooked through. Stir in the shawarma spice and cook for a further 1 minute.

Lightly toast the pitta bread. Mix the tahini with the honey, vinegar and hot water in a small bowl. Season lightly with salt and pepper.

Shred the lettuce on a plate and pile the chicken mixture on top. Scatter with the gherkin and spoon over the tahini dressing. Serve with the toasted pitta bread.

Mustard Rarebit

SERVES 4

25 g (1 oz) butter
4 spring onions, thinly sliced
250 g (8 oz) Cheddar or Red Leicester cheese, grated
50 ml (2 fl oz) beer
2 teaspoons mustard
4 slices of wholemeal bread
pepper
salad, to serve (optional)

Heat the butter in a frying pan, add the spring onions and fry for 5 minutes or until softened.

Reduce the heat to low and stir in the cheese, beer and mustard. Season well with pepper, then stir slowly for 3–4 minutes or until the cheese has melted.

Meanwhile, toast the bread lightly on both sides and place on a grill pan. Pour the cheese mixture over the toast and cook under a preheated hot grill for 1 minute or until bubbling and golden. Serve with a salad, if liked.

snacks & sides

Very Versatile DIY Falafels

£ Vegan >50

MAKES 30

400 g (13 oz) dried chickpeas
150 g (5 oz) fava beans or dried broad beans
large handful of coriander
large handful of flat leaf parsley
large handful of spinach (about 50 g/2 oz)
1 red onion, quartered
3 garlic cloves
2 teaspoons ground cumin
2 teaspoons ground coriander
finely grated zest and juice of 1 lemon
1 tablespoon baking powder
flavourless oil, for deep-frying
salt and pepper

Place the chickpeas and fava or broad beans in a very large bowl and cover generously with cold water. Leave overnight to soak; they will double in size.

The next morning, drain and rinse them well and put them in a food processor with the herbs, spinach, onion and garlic. Blitz until fully combined but still with some crumbly texture.

Tip the mixture out into a large bowl and add the ground spices, lemon zest and juice. Season to taste. If you're making the falafel straight away, add the baking powder (this should always be the last step before shaping to ensure you get lovely puffy and light falafel).

Shape the mixture into balls or pucks, using around 2 tablespoons of mixture for each.

Heat enough oil for frying in a deep saucepan, about 3.5 cm (1½ inches) deep, over a medium-high heat until the oil shimmers. Carefully add the falafel in batches, 5–6 at a time, and fry for 6–8 minutes, turning regularly to get an even, deep golden-brown colour. Drain on kitchen paper, season with salt and keep warm to enjoy hot or allow to cool to room temperature.

Store in an airtight container in the refrigerator for up to 5 days.

Falafels with Beetroot Salad & Mint Yogurt

SERVES 2

FALAFELS

400 g (13 oz) can chickpeas, rinsed and drained
½ small red onion, roughly chopped
1 garlic clove, chopped
½ red chilli, deseeded
1 teaspoon ground cumin
1 teaspoon ground coriander
handful of flat leaf parsley
2 tablespoons olive oil
salt and pepper

BEETROOT SALAD

1 carrot, coarsely grated
1 raw beetroot, coarsely grated
50 g (2 oz) baby spinach leaves
1 tablespoon lemon juice
2 tablespoons olive oil

MINT YOGURT

150 ml (¼ pint) 0%-fat Greek yogurt
1 tablespoon chopped mint leaves
½ garlic clove, crushed

To make the falafels, place the chickpeas, onion, garlic, chilli, cumin, coriander and parsley in a blender or food processor. Season with salt and pepper, then process to make a coarse paste. Shape the mixture into 8 patties and set aside.

To make the salad, place the carrot, beetroot and spinach in a bowl. Season with salt and pepper, add the lemon juice and oil and stir well.

To make the mint yogurt, mix all the ingredients together in a small bowl and season with a little salt.

Heat the oil in a frying pan, add the falafels and fry for 4–5 minutes on each side until golden. Serve with the beetroot salad and mint yogurt.

Sweetcorn & Onion Pakoras

SERVES 4

300 g (10 oz) sweetcorn
4 spring onions, finely sliced
1 green chilli, deseeded and finely chopped
large handful of coriander, finely chopped, plus extra to serve
1 tablespoon garam masala
100 g (3½ oz) plain flour or gram (chickpea) flour
1 teaspoon salt, plus extra to serve
mango chutney, to serve (optional)
flavourless oil, for deep-frying

TIP

The gentle spice is wonderful in these miniature crispy pakoras. If you don't have a green chilli or any coriander, just add ½ teaspoon each of chilli powder and ground coriander.

Mix the sweetcorn, spring onions, chilli, coriander, garam masala, flour and salt in a large bowl. Stir together, adding 2–3 tablespoons of water until the batter is just wet enough to cling together.

Heat 3.5 cm (1½ inches) of oil in a large saucepan over a medium heat until the oil shimmers. Spoon tablespoonfuls of the thick batter directly into the oil in batches, 4–5 at a time, and cook for 3–4 minutes until golden brown.

Drain on kitchen paper, then serve hot, with an extra sprinkling of salt and coriander, and mango chutney, if you like, while you cook the remaining pakoras.

Salmon & Rice Bhajis

££ | **Veggie** | **>20**

SERVES 4

2 x 170 g (6 oz) cans salmon, drained and flaked
1 small onion, sliced
½ teaspoon ground cumin
¼ teaspoon dried chilli flakes
2 tablespoons chopped coriander
75 g (3 oz) cooked cold white rice
1 egg, beaten
1–2 tablespoons plain flour
2 tablespoons flavourless oil
150 ml (¼ pint) natural yogurt
½ cucumber, grated
1 tablespoon chopped mint
salt and pepper

Place the salmon, onion, spices, coriander and rice in a large bowl and mix well. Stir in the egg and season well with salt and pepper. Mix in enough of the flour to form a stiff mixture. Using wet hands, shape into 20 small balls.

Heat the oil in a large frying pan, add the bhajis and fry for 3–4 minutes, turning once, until golden.

Meanwhile, mix together the yogurt, cucumber and mint in a bowl. Serve with the hot bhajis.

Any Vegetable Bhajis

SERVES 4

200 g (7 oz) gram (chickpea) flour
175 ml (6 fl oz) warm water
small handful of coriander, very finely chopped
1 small green chilli, deseeded and very finely chopped
1 teaspoon ground turmeric
1 teaspoon ground cumin
1 teaspoon chilli powder
flavourless oil, for deep-frying
500 g (1 lb) vegetables of your choice, finely sliced
salt and pepper
mango chutney, to serve (optional)

TIP

One of the best ways to make cheap vegetables go further, taste more delicious and satisfy a crowd is to deep-fry them in a crunchy coating. It's not rocket science. Once you've mastered bhaji batter, you can fry any sturdy-ish vegetables. Try thinly sliced onion, carrot, courgette, broccoli, kohlrabi, cauliflower, Brussels sprouts, kale... you name it. They will work mixed together or you can be a purist about it. You can even 'bhaji' old herb stems and salad leaves. The possibilities are endless.

Put the gram flour into a large bowl. Add most of the measured water and whisk well to combine. You may not need all of the water – add just enough to give a batter the consistency of double cream.

Whisk in the coriander, chilli and ground spices and season well with salt and pepper.

Heat the oil in a large saucepan over a medium heat, filling the pan no more than half full, until the oil shimmers.

Dip the sliced vegetables in the batter, stir, then lower spoonfuls of them carefully into the hot oil. Fry in batches, for a few minutes, turning regularly to get an even golden-brown colour.

Remove with a slotted spoon and drain on kitchen paper. If some of the batter has come away from the bhajis, simply fish it out and serve with the bhajis. Eat the bhajis hot, with mango chutney, if you like.

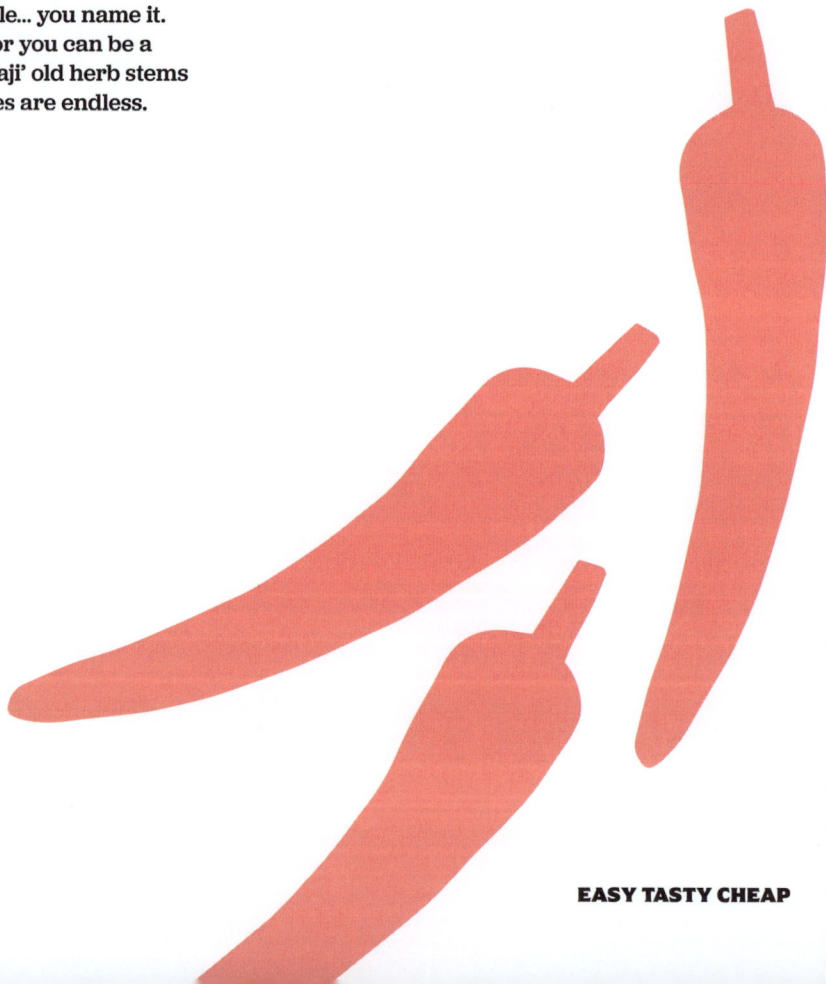

Spicy Courgette Fritters

££ Veggie

>50

SERVES 4

3 courgettes
2 large spring onions, grated or very finely chopped
1 garlic clove, finely chopped
finely grated zest of 1 lemon
4 tablespoons gram (chickpea) flour
2 teaspoons medium curry powder
1 red chilli, deseeded and finely chopped
2 tablespoons finely chopped mint leaves
2 tablespoons finely chopped fresh coriander leaves
2 eggs, lightly beaten
2 tablespoons light olive oil
salt and pepper

Grate the courgettes into a colander. Sprinkle lightly with salt and leave for at least 1 hour to drain. Squeeze out the remaining liquid.

Place the remaining ingredients, except the eggs and oil, in a mixing bowl and add the grated courgettes. Season lightly with salt and pepper, bearing in mind you have already salted the courgettes, and mix well. Add the eggs and mix again to combine.

Heat half of the oil in a large frying pan over a medium-high heat. Place dessert spoonfuls of the mixture (in batches), well spaced, in the pan and press down with the back of the spoon. Cook for 1–2 minutes on each side, until golden and cooked through. Remove from the pan and keep warm. Repeat to cook the rest of the fritters in the same way, adding the remaining oil to the pan when necessary. Serve warm.

Vegetable Crisps

£ Vegan

<20

SERVES 6

300 g (10 oz) sweet potatoes, raw beetroot, carrots or parsnips, peeled
3 tablespoons olive oil
salt and pepper

Use a vegetable peeler to create strips of the vegetables or slice them finely. Place on a baking sheet.

Toss with the oil and season well. Bake in a preheated oven, 180°C (350°F), Gas Mark 4, for 10–15 minutes in an even layer, turning once during cooking, until crisp and golden. Allow to cool completely on the baking sheet. Once cool, these will keep in an airtight container for up to 1 week.

Curried Leek & Potato Puffs

MAKES 6

½ quantity Roasted Leeks & Potatoes (see 85)
75 g (3 oz) frozen peas, defrosted
1 tablespoon lemon or lime juice
1 tablespoon curry powder
500 g (1 lb) block of vegan puff pastry
a little plain flour, for dusting
2 tablespoons dairy-free milk
1 tablespoon sesame seeds
salt and pepper

TIP
These Indian-spiced curry puffs are ideal to take on a picnic or for a packed lunch.

In a medium-sized bowl, lightly mash the roasted leeks and potatoes, leaving some large chunks. Fold in the peas, lemon or lime juice and curry powder. Season and set aside.

On a lightly floured surface, roll out the puff pastry into a large square (about 35 cm/14 inch). Cut it in half, then cut each half into 3 to give 6 rectangles. Roll each rectangle out a little more to give you a squarer shape of thinner pastry.

Heap 1–2 tablespoons of filling in the centre of each pastry square and fold one corner in diagonally over the filling, making a triangular-shaped pasty. Using your finger or a pastry brush, put some dairy-free milk on the seam to help you to seal it, push gently with your fingers, then crimp with your fingers or a fork to seal tightly.

Repeat with the remaining pastry squares and filling, then brush all over with dairy-free milk and sprinkle with sesame seeds.

Bake in a preheated oven, 190°C (375°F), Gas Mark 5, on a large baking tray for 30–35 minutes.

Mini Hummus & Carrot Tarts

SERVES 4

320 g (11 oz) sheet ready-rolled vegan puff pastry
1 tablespoon dairy-free milk
1 quantity Any Can Hummus (see page 210)
1 quantity Maple Roast Carrots (see page 74)
50 g (2 oz) green olives, pitted and halved
50 g (2 oz) pomegranate seeds (optional)
large handful of flat leaf parsley, finely chopped

Cut the sheet of puff pastry into 4 rectangles and place on a large baking tray. Score a 2.5 cm (1 inch) border around each edge and prick the centres with a fork. Brush the outer edges with the milk. Bake in a preheated oven, 190°C (375°F), Gas Mark 5, for 12–15 minutes until risen and golden. Remove from the oven and push down the centre rectangles with the back of a spoon.

Spread the hummus in the centre of each tart, top with the carrots and olives and return to the oven for 5 minutes to warm through. Scatter the tarts with the pomegranate seeds, if using, and parsley before serving.

TIP
You can swap the hummus for pesto or use any roasted vegetables instead of the carrots.

Spiced Chicken & Mango Salad

££   **<20**

SERVES 4

6 teaspoons mild curry paste
juice of 1 lemon
4 small boneless, skinless chicken breasts, cut
  into long, thin strips
150 g (5 oz) natural yogurt
1 ripe mango, peeled, pitted and cut into bite-sized
  chunks
50 g (2 oz) watercress, torn into smaller pieces
½ cucumber, diced
½ red onion, chopped
½ iceberg lettuce

Put 4 teaspoons of the curry paste into a plastic food bag with the lemon juice and mix together by squeezing the bag. Add the chicken strips and toss together.

Half-fill the base of a steamer with water and bring to the boil. Remove the chicken from the bag and place in the top of the steamer in a single layer. Cover and steam for 5–6 minutes until cooked through.

Meanwhile, mix the remaining curry paste in a bowl with the yogurt. Put the mango, watercress, cucumber and onion in a bowl, add the yogurt dressing and toss together gently.

Tear the lettuce into pieces, divide it between 4 plates, then spoon the mango mixture on top. Add the warm chicken strips on top, then serve.

VARIATION

For **coronation chicken**, mix the curry paste and yogurt with 4 tablespoons of mayonnaise. Stir in 500 g (1 lb) cold cooked diced chicken and 40 g (1½ oz) sultanas. Sprinkle with 25 g (1 oz) toasted flaked almonds and serve on a bed of mixed salad and herb leaves.

Fattoush Salad

SERVES 4

1 pitta bread, torn into small pieces
6 plum tomatoes, deseeded and roughly chopped
1 cucumber, peeled and roughly chopped
10 radishes, sliced
1 red onion, roughly chopped
1 small Little Gem lettuce, leaves separated
small handful of fresh mint leaves

DRESSING

200 ml (7 fl oz) olive oil
juice of 3 lemons
1 garlic clove, crushed
2 teaspoons sumac or 2 teaspoons ground cumin
salt and pepper

First make the dressing. Whisk the oil, lemon juice, garlic and sumac or cumin together in a bowl. Season to taste with salt and pepper.

To make the salad, combine the pitta pieces, tomatoes, cucumber, radishes, onion, lettuce leaves and mint leaves in a large bowl.

Pour the dressing over the salad and gently mix together to coat the salad evenly.

Courgette, Feta & Mint Salad

SERVES 2

3 green courgettes
2 yellow courgettes
olive oil, for drizzling
small bunch of mint leaves
40 g (1½ oz) feta cheese
salt and pepper

DRESSING

2 tablespoons olive oil
finely grated zest and juice of 1 lemon

Thinly slice the courgettes lengthways into long ribbons. Drizzle with oil and season with salt and pepper. Heat a griddle pan until it's very hot, then grill the courgettes, in batches, until tender and griddle-marked on both sides. Transfer to a large salad bowl.

Make the dressing by whisking together the oil and lemon zest and juice in a small bowl. Season to taste with salt and pepper.

Roughly chop the mint, reserving some leaves for the garnish. Carefully mix together the griddled courgettes, chopped mint and dressing in the salad bowl, then crumble the feta over the top, garnish with the remaining mint leaves and serve.

Soy Tofu Salad with Coriander

£ Vegan <20

SERVES 4

500 g (1 lb) firm tofu, drained
6 spring onions, finely shredded
large handful of coriander leaves,
  roughly chopped
1 large mild red chilli, deseeded and thinly sliced
4 tablespoons light soy sauce
2 teaspoons sesame oil

Cut the tofu into bite-sized cubes and carefully arrange on a serving plate in a single layer. Sprinkle over the spring onions, coriander and chilli.

Drizzle over the soy sauce and oil, then leave to stand at room temperature for 10 minutes before serving.

VARIATION

For **steamed chilli-soy tofu**, drain 500 g (1 lb) firm tofu, cut it into bite-sized cubes and place it on a heatproof plate that will fit inside a bamboo steamer. Cover and steam over a wok or large saucepan of boiling water for 20 minutes, then drain off the excess water and carefully transfer to a serving plate. Heat 4 tablespoons light soy sauce, 1 tablespoon each sesame oil and groundnut oil and 2 teaspoons oyster sauce in a small saucepan until hot. Pour over the tofu, scatter with 4 thinly sliced spring onions, 1 finely chopped red chilli and a small handful of finely chopped coriander leaves and serve.

Carrot Top Pesto & Couscous Salad

SERVES 2

CARROT TOP PESTO

1 bunch of carrot tops
large handful of flat leaf parsley
large handful of coriander
5 tablespoons olive oil, or any flavourless oil
3 tablespoons water, plus extra if needed
1 teaspoon ground cumin
1 teaspoon ground coriander
1 green chilli, deseeded and roughly chopped

COUSCOUS SALAD

200 g (7 oz) couscous
2 tablespoons olive oil
finely grated zest and juice of 1 lemon
½ quantity Maple Roast Carrots (see page 74)
40 g (1½ oz) flaked almonds
handful of pomegranate seeds (optional)
salt and pepper

Blitz all the ingredients for the pesto in a blender or food processor until fully combined. Add a splash more water if it seems too thick.

Place the couscous in a heatproof bowl with just enough boiling water to cover. Cover the bowl and set aside for 5 minutes to absorb the water.

Fluff up the couscous with a fork, season with salt and pepper and add the olive oil, lemon zest and juice.

Top the couscous with the carrots, drizzle with the pesto and scatter with flaked almonds and pomegranate seeds, if using.

TIP

This recipe makes use of the leafy greens on top of bunched carrots that are typically thrown away. If your carrots didn't come with any, use spinach or any other soft leafy greens, or extra herbs, in their place. The pesto has a Middle Eastern flavour with plenty of kick. Swap the couscous here for rice, bulgur wheat, quinoa or any other grain you have on hand.

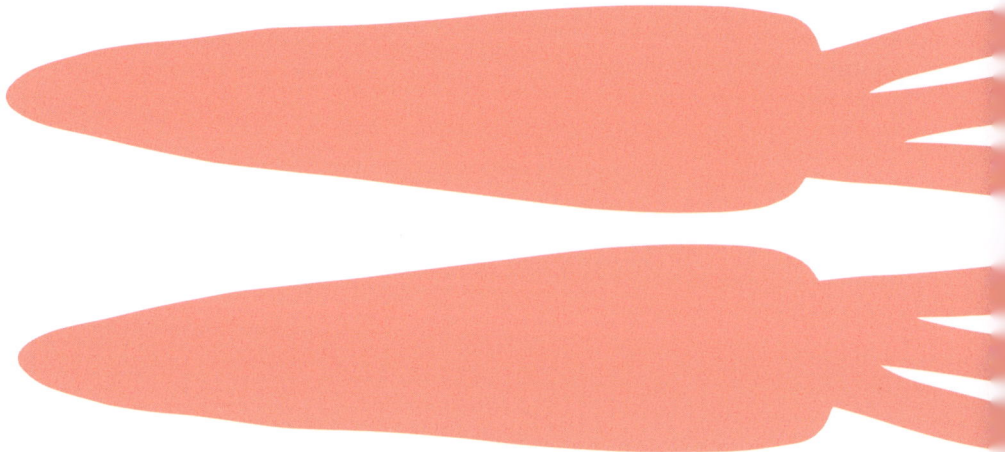

Roasted Veggie & Quinoa Salad

SERVES 4

3 courgettes, cut into chunks
2 red peppers, cored, deseeded and cut
  into chunks
2 red onions, cut into wedges
1 large aubergine, cut into chunks
3 garlic cloves
3 tablespoons olive oil
150 g (5 oz) quinoa
2 tablespoons green pesto or sun-dried
  tomato paste
1 tablespoon balsamic vinegar
75 g (3 oz) rocket

Put all the vegetables and garlic on a large baking sheet and drizzle over the olive oil. Place in a preheated oven, 220°C (425°F), Gas Mark 7, for 20–25 minutes until tender and beginning to char.

Cook the quinoa, meanwhile, in a saucepan of boiling water according to the pack instructions, then drain well.

Whisk together the pesto or tomato paste and balsamic vinegar in a small bowl. Place the roasted vegetables, rocket and quinoa in a large bowl and stir in the dressing. Serve warm.

TIP
Equally delicious served cold, any leftovers can be popped in a lidded container for a quick portable lunch.

Veggie Niçoise Salad

SERVES 4

400 g (13 oz) small potatoes
200 g (7 oz) green beans, trimmed
5 large plum tomatoes
2 tablespoons chopped parsley, plus extra leaves
  to garnish
60 g (2¼ oz) pitted black olives
2 tablespoons lemon juice
2 tablespoons olive oil, plus extra to drizzle
4 large, soft-poached eggs
salt and pepper

Cook the potatoes in lightly salted boiling water, leave them to cool and halve them. Meanwhile, bring a large saucepan of lightly salted water to the boil, add the trimmed green beans and cook for 1—2 minutes until bright green and still firm to the touch. Refresh in cold water, drain and transfer to a large salad bowl.

Core the tomatoes and cut each one into 6 pieces. Add the tomatoes and chopped parsley to the beans with the potatoes, olives, lemon juice and oil. Season to taste with salt and pepper.

Transfer the salad to plates and top each one with a poached egg cut in half and a drizzle of olive oil. Garnish with the reserved parsley leaves and serve.

Smoked Mackerel Superfood Salad

££ >20

SERVES 4

500 g (1 lb) butternut squash, peeled, deseeded
  and cut into 1 cm (½ inch) cubes
4 tablespoons olive oil
1 teaspoon cumin seeds
1 head of broccoli, cut into florets
200 g (7 oz) frozen or fresh peas
3 tablespoons quinoa
4 tablespoons mixed seeds
2 smoked mackerel fillets
juice of 1 lemon
½ teaspoon honey
½ teaspoon Dijon mustard
100 g (3½ oz) red cabbage, shredded
4 tomatoes, chopped
4 cooked beetroot, cut into wedges
20 g (¾ oz) radish sprouts

Place the squash in a roasting tin and sprinkle with 1 tablespoon of the olive oil and the cumin seeds. Place in a preheated oven, 200°C (400°F), Gas Mark 6, for 15–18 minutes until tender. Leave to cool slightly.

Meanwhile, cook the broccoli in boiling water for 4–5 minutes until tender, adding the peas 3 minutes before the end of the cooking time. Remove with a slotted spoon and refresh under cold running water, then drain. Cook the quinoa in the broccoli water for 15 minutes, then drain and leave to cool slightly.

Heat a nonstick frying pan over a medium-low heat and dry-fry the seeds, stirring frequently, until golden brown and toasted; set aside. Heat the mackerel fillets according to the pack instructions. Skin and break into flakes.

Whisk together the remaining olive oil, lemon juice, honey and mustard in a small bowl. Toss together all the ingredients, except the radish sprouts, with the dressing in a large bowl. Serve topped with the sprouts.

Brainfood Bowl

SERVES 2

100 g (3½ oz) brown rice
150 g (5 oz) broccoli florets
75 g (3 oz) sugar snap peas, halved lengthways
50 g (2 oz) hazelnuts, roughly chopped
25 g (1 oz) pumpkin seeds
1 pink or red grapefruit
1 ripe avocado
25 g (1 oz) fresh root ginger, peeled and grated
1 tablespoon olive oil
1 tablespoon honey
salt and pepper

Cook the rice in a large saucepan of lightly salted water for 25 minutes or until just tender.

Meanwhile, cut the broccoli into smaller pieces and cook in a separate saucepan of boiling water for 2 minutes until softened. Add the sugar snap peas and cook for a further 30 seconds. Drain, rinse under cold running water, then drain again.

Lightly toast the hazelnuts in a dry frying pan, shaking the pan frequently until the nuts start to colour. Add the pumpkin seeds and cook for a further 1–2 minutes until they start to pop.

Thoroughly drain the rice and mix in a bowl with the broccoli, sugar snap peas, nuts and seeds.

Halve the grapefruit. Squeeze the juice from one half into a small bowl. Cut away the skin and white pith from the remaining half and chop the flesh. Add to the rice bowl. Peel, pit and dice the avocado and add to the grapefruit juice. Toss to coat, then lift out with a slotted spoon and add to the rice.

Whisk the ginger, oil and honey into the grapefruit juice. Stir the dressing into the rice mixture just before serving. Season to taste with salt and pepper and serve.

Chicken Couscous Salad

£ £   > 50

SERVES 4

4 boneless, skinless chicken breasts, each about
125 g (4 oz)
300 g (10 oz) couscous
300 ml (½ pint) hot chicken stock (see page 197)
1 pomegranate
zest and juice of 1 orange
small bunch of coriander
small bunch of mint

MARINADE

1½ tablespoons tikka masala curry paste
5 tablespoons natural yogurt
1 teaspoon olive oil
2 tablespoons lemon juice

Make a marinade by mixing the curry paste, yogurt and oil. Put the chicken in a non-metallic dish, cover with half the marinade and leave for at least 1 hour.

Put the couscous in a bowl, add the hot stock, cover and leave for 8 minutes.

Meanwhile, cut the pomegranate in half and remove the seeds. Add them to the couscous with the orange zest and juice.

Remove the chicken from the marinade, reserving the marinade, and transfer to a foil-lined baking sheet. Cook in a preheated oven, 190°C (375°F), Gas Mark 5, for 6–7 minutes, then transfer to a preheated hot grill and cook for 2 minutes until caramelized. Cover with foil and leave to rest for 5 minutes.

Roughly chop the coriander and mint, reserving some whole coriander leaves for garnish, and add to the couscous. Thinly slice the chicken. Spoon the couscous on to plates and add the chicken. Thin the reserved marinade with the lemon juice and drizzle over the couscous. Garnish with the reserved coriander leaves and serve immediately.

Balsamic Roast Veg Salad

SERVES 4

1 red onion, roughly chopped

4 carrots, roughly chopped

1 red pepper, cored, deseeded and cut into large pieces

1 sweet potato, peeled and cut into even-sized pieces

400 g (13 oz) courgettes, cut into even-sized pieces

1 butternut squash, about 1 kg (2 lb), peeled, deseeded and cut into chunks

2 tablespoons olive oil, plus extra to drizzle

150 ml (¼ pint) balsamic vinegar

1 tablespoon chopped thyme

1 tablespoon chopped rosemary

75 g (3 oz) rocket

salt and pepper

Put all the vegetables in a roasting tin, drizzle over the oil and balsamic vinegar and sprinkle with the herbs. Toss to make sure everything is well coated in the oil, then season to taste. Roast in a preheated oven, 190°C (375°F), Gas Mark 5, for 30 minutes, or until they are cooked and slightly crispy.

Remove the vegetables from the oven, allow to cool slightly, then toss with the rocket. Drizzle with olive oil, check the seasoning and serve.

TIP

Student freezers are often filled with more ice than food. Don't wait until you can't shut the door: a regular defrost will help the freezer run more economically and maximize the storage space. This is a great revision-avoidance job.

Chickpea Tabbouleh

£   Vegan   >20

SERVES 2

400 g (13 oz) can chickpeas, drained and rinsed
1 tablespoon ras el hanout
2 tablespoons olive oil
200 g (7 oz) couscous
1 tablespoon vegan bouillon powder
1 orange, zest finely grated, fruit segmented
1 carrot, grated
1 cucumber, grated
½ red onion, finely chopped
6 radishes, finely sliced
large handful of flat leaf parsley, roughly chopped
large handful of coriander, roughly chopped

Dry the drained chickpeas thoroughly, tip on to a baking tray and toss with the ras el hanout and oil. Roast in a preheated oven, 190°C (375°F), Gas Mark 5, for 10–15 minutes until crisp.

Meanwhile, put the couscous in a large heatproof bowl and stir in the bouillon powder until evenly combined. Pour over just enough boiling water to cover the couscous, then cover the bowl with a plate or clingfilm for 5–8 minutes until the couscous has absorbed all the liquid.

To assemble the tabbouleh, fluff up the couscous with a fork and stir in the orange zest and segments, carrot, cucumber, red onion, radishes and herbs. Top with the crispy chickpeas and enjoy.

TIP
Make a double batch of the crispy chickpeas, because on their own they're a great snack and much healthier than crisps. The trick to these crispy chickpeas is to dry them thoroughly before baking. The spices make a real impact on the flavour – try smoked paprika, cumin, garam masala or ground coriander.

£ | Vegan

Crispy Chickpeas

>20

SERVES 6

400 g (13 oz) can chickpeas, drained and rinsed
2 tablespoons extra virgin olive oil or regular olive oil
1 teaspoon spice of your choice (see tip on page 73)

Preheat the oven to 190°C (375°F), Gas Mark 5.

Dry the chickpeas thoroughly, then toss with the olive oil and your chosen spice on a large baking sheet (they need lots of space around them to crisp up).

Bake for 20 minutes until crisp and golden.

£ | Vegan

Maple Roast Carrots

>20

SERVES 4

1 bunch of carrots, preferably with green leafy tops (total weight about 1 kg/2 lb), peeled and halved
2 tablespoons olive oil
2 tablespoons maple syrup
salt and pepper

Toss the carrots with the olive oil on a large baking tray and spread them out in an even layer – you want to roast them, not steam them, so they need space to caramelize. Season with salt and pepper and roast in a preheated oven, 190°C (375°F), Gas Mark 5, for 30–35 minutes until golden and soft to the touch.

Drizzle over the maple syrup and return to the oven for 5 minutes, until the carrots are sticky and smell fragrant.

Enjoy warm, or leave to cool, then store in an airtight container in the refrigerator for up to 5 days.

TIP

Carrots are one of the cheapest vegetables out there and roasting them brings out their wonderfully sweet flavour, which gets a helping hand here from a splash of maple syrup to make them sticky and moreish. They keep really well, so if you roast a bunch of carrots, you can use them in meals for the rest of the week. You can leave out the maple syrup and try using any herbs and spices you have in the cupboard if you prefer.

Harissa Bean Mash & Roasted Carrots

<20

SERVES 2

400 g (13 oz) can butter beans or other
   white beans
2 tablespoons olive oil
finely grated zest and juice of 1 lemon
1 tablespoon harissa
½ quantity Maple Roast Carrots (see opposite)
small handful of coriander, finely chopped,
   to serve
salt and pepper

Pour the can of beans, with its liquid, into a small, deep saucepan. Bring to a simmer, then add the olive oil, lemon juice and harissa and mash well with a fork, or use a hand blender to get it super creamy and smooth. You can add a splash of water if you want it to be a bit looser.

Spoon the mash in to a serving dish, top it with the carrots and lemon zest, season well and sprinkle with coriander.

Caramelized Parsnips

>20

SERVES 2

625 g (1¼ lb) parsnips, scrubbed or peeled
50 g (2 oz) butter
175 g (6 oz) diced bacon
3 tablespoons caster sugar
50 g (2 oz) pine nuts
5 tablespoons chopped thyme

Cut the parsnips in half widthways, then cut the chunky tops into quarters lengthways and the slim bottom halves in half lengthways.

Heat the butter in a large frying pan, add the bacon and parsnips and cook over a medium heat for about 15 minutes, turning and tossing occasionally, until the parsnips are golden and softened and the bacon is crisp.

Add the sugar and pine nuts and cook for a further 2–3 minutes until lightly caramelized. Toss with the thyme and serve.

Cauliflower Nuggets

SERVES 2

1 medium cauliflower, broken into florets
4 tablespoons cornflour
1 tablespoon smoked paprika
1 teaspoon ground coriander
4 tablespoons dairy-free milk
100 g (3½ oz) panko breadcrumbs or regular very
   dry breadcrumbs
4 tablespoons flavourless oil
salt and pepper

TO SERVE

small handful of finely chopped chives (optional)
hot sauce

Steam or boil the cauliflower in salted water for 5 minutes until almost tender. Drain well and transfer to a large baking tray.

Sprinkle the cornflour and spices over the florets and toss to coat.

Pour over the dairy-free milk and toss to coat again, followed by the breadcrumbs, tossing a final time to make sure every crevice is covered in breadcrumbs. Season well with salt and pepper.

Drizzle the oil over the breadcrumbed florets and bake in a preheated oven, 200°C (400°F), Gas Mark 6, for 15 minutes until the breadcrumbs are deeply golden and the cauliflower is cooked through. Serve with chopped chives, if you like, and hot sauce.

TIP

Irresistibly crunchy and so simple to make – there's no time wasted breadcrumbing the individual cauliflower florets. Mixing the wet ingredients and breadcrumbs on the baking tray means you get lots of extra crispy morsels of flavoured breadcrumb shards to serve with the nuggets. Switch up the spices if you fancy a change – these would be wonderful in a traditional fast-food style with onion and garlic powder or given an Indian twist with garam masala and ground cumin.

Cauliflower Cheese

£ Veggie <20

SERVES 4
1 large cauliflower, broken into pieces
50 g (2 oz) butter
4 tablespoons plain flour
½ teaspoon English mustard powder
500 ml (17 fl oz) milk
100 g (3½ oz) mature Cheddar cheese, grated
2 tablespoons pumpkin seeds

Cook the cauliflower in a large saucepan of boiling water for 5–6 minutes until tender.

Meanwhile, melt the butter in a small saucepan, then stir in the flour and mustard powder to make a smooth paste. Cook for 1–2 minutes, then gradually whisk in the milk. Cook, stirring continuously, until the sauce is thick and smooth. Simmer for 1 minute, then stir in half the cheese.

Drain the cauliflower and place in an ovenproof dish. Pour over the cheese sauce, then sprinkle with the pumpkin seeds and remaining cheese. Cook under a preheated hot grill for 2–3 minutes until bubbling and golden.

Quick Spinach with Pine Nuts

SERVES 4

1 tablespoon olive oil
1 red onion, sliced
1 garlic clove, crushed
75 g (3 oz) pine nuts
4 tomatoes, skinned, cored and roughly chopped
1 kg (2 lb) spinach
50 g (2 oz) butter
pinch of freshly grated nutmeg
salt and pepper

Heat the oil in a large saucepan, add the onion and garlic and fry for 5 minutes.

Put the pine nuts into a small, heavy-based frying pan and dry-fry until browned, stirring constantly as they turn brown very quickly. Remove from the heat.

Add the tomatoes, spinach, butter and nutmeg to the onion and garlic and season with salt and pepper. Turn up the heat to high and mix well. Cook for 3 minutes until the spinach has just started to wilt, stirring frequently.

Remove from the heat, stir in the pine nuts and serve immediately.

Courgette & Ricotta Bakes

SERVES 4

butter, for greasing
2 courgettes
100 g (3½ oz) fresh white or wholemeal breadcrumbs
250 g (8 oz) ricotta cheese
75 g (3 oz) Parmesan-style cheese, grated
2 eggs, beaten
1 garlic clove, crushed
handful of chopped basil
salt and pepper

Grease 8 holes of a muffin tin.

Use a vegetable peeler to make 16 long ribbons of courgette and set aside. Coarsely grate the remaining courgettes and squeeze to remove any excess moisture. Mix the grated courgettes with all the remaining ingredients in a bowl and season well with salt and pepper.

Arrange 2 courgette ribbons in a cross shape in each hole of the prepared muffin tin. Spoon in the filling and then fold over the overhanging courgette ends. Bake in a preheated oven, 190°C (375°F), Gas Mark 5, for 15–20 minutes or until golden and cooked through. Turn out on to plates and serve immediately.

VARIATION

For **mushrooms stuffed with courgettes and ricotta**, brush a little olive oil over 4 large field mushrooms, trimmed, and place on a baking tray, stalk-side up. Grate 1 courgette and squeeze to remove any excess moisture, then mix with 200 g (7 oz) ricotta cheese, 4 drained and chopped sun-dried tomatoes in oil and 25 g (1 oz) chopped pitted black olives. Season with salt and pepper, spoon on to the mushrooms, then sprinkle with 25 g (1 oz) grated Parmesan-style cheese. Bake in a preheated oven, 200°C (400°F), Gas Mark 6, for 15 minutes until golden and cooked through. Serve with ciabatta rolls.

£ · Vegan · <20

Courgette Satay

SERVES 2

SKEWERS

2 courgettes, cut into 3 cm (1¼ inches) chunks
1 teaspoon ground turmeric
1 tablespoon soy sauce
1 tablespoon sesame oil or flavourless oil

SATAY SAUCE

3 tablespoons crunchy peanut butter
5 tablespoons coconut milk
1 tablespoon soy sauce
1 tablespoon caster sugar
1 tablespoon lime juice

TO SERVE

carrot shavings
cucumber slices
thinly sliced red onion
1 red chilli, deseeded and finely sliced
small handful of coriander, roughly chopped
small handful of mint leaves

Soak 6 bamboo skewers in water to prevent them burning later on.

Preheat a large griddle or frying pan. In a bowl, toss the courgettes with the turmeric, soy sauce and oil. Lay them out in a single layer in the pan and cook for 3–4 minutes on each side until caramelized and soft.

Meanwhile, whisk together the satay sauce ingredients and microwave on high for 30 seconds to help it come together smoothly, then stir.

Serve the skewers with lots of fresh crunchy salad – carrot, cucumber, red onion and red chilli – with coriander and mint scattered over and the satay sauce in a bowl on the side.

TIP

These vegetable skewers are really versatile – try replacing the courgette with aubergine, sweet potato or any squash. The sauce will appear to split after first mixing it but, after flashing it in the microwave, it should come together. If you don't have skewers, just griddle or fry the courgettes.

£ · Veggie · >20

Stuffed Courgettes

SERVES 4

4 courgettes
175 g (6 oz) plum tomatoes, chopped
200 g (7 oz) mozzarella cheese, grated
2 tablespoons shredded basil
25 g (1 oz) Parmesan-style cheese, grated
salt and pepper

Slice the courgettes in half horizontally and then scoop out the middle of each one, reserving the flesh. Place the courgette halves, cut-side up, in a roasting tin and bake in a preheated oven, 200°C (400°F), Gas Mark 6, for 10 minutes.

Meanwhile, to make the filling, chop the reserved courgette flesh and mix it in a bowl with the tomatoes, mozzarella and basil. Season to taste with salt and pepper.

Remove the courgette halves from the oven and spoon the filling into each one. Sprinkle with the Parmesan-style cheese and return to the oven for 15 minutes, or until golden.

Smashed Cucumber & Radishes

££ · Vegan · **<20**

SERVES 2

1 cucumber, roughly peeled
250 g (8 oz) radishes
2 tablespoons crispy chilli oil, plus extra (optional) for drizzling
2 tablespoons soy sauce
1 tablespoon caster sugar
½ quantity Avocado Crema (optional, see page 212)
sesame seeds, to serve

Use a large knife to roughly chop the cucumbers and halve the radishes, then cover each piece with the flat of the knife and use the heel of your hand to press down. Place the smashed pieces in a bowl and toss with the chilli oil, soy sauce and sugar.

Spread the Avocado Crema, if using, on a serving plate and top with the smashed cucumbers and radishes and all the sauce. Serve with more chilli oil, if you like things spicy, and sesame seeds.

TIP

This dish is at its best when using a proper Chinese crispy chilli oil, the kind with lots of crunchy bits in.

Chilli Kale

£ · Vegan · **<20**

SERVES 4

1 tablespoon olive oil
1 garlic clove, crushed
1 large onion, chopped
500 g (1 lb) kale, stalks removed and leaves chopped
2 teaspoons lime juice
1 red chilli, deseeded and chopped
salt and pepper

Heat the oil in a wok or large frying pan over a medium heat. Add the garlic and onion and stir-fry for 5–10 minutes or until the onion is translucent.

Add the kale and stir-fry for a further 5 minutes. Stir in the lime juice and chilli, season with salt and pepper to taste and then serve immediately.

VARIATION

For chilli cabbage, replace the curly kale with 500 g (1 lb) cabbage. Discard the stalks and tough outer leaves, then chop the leaves before frying with the softened garlic and onion, then finishing as above. This recipe also works well with spring greens.

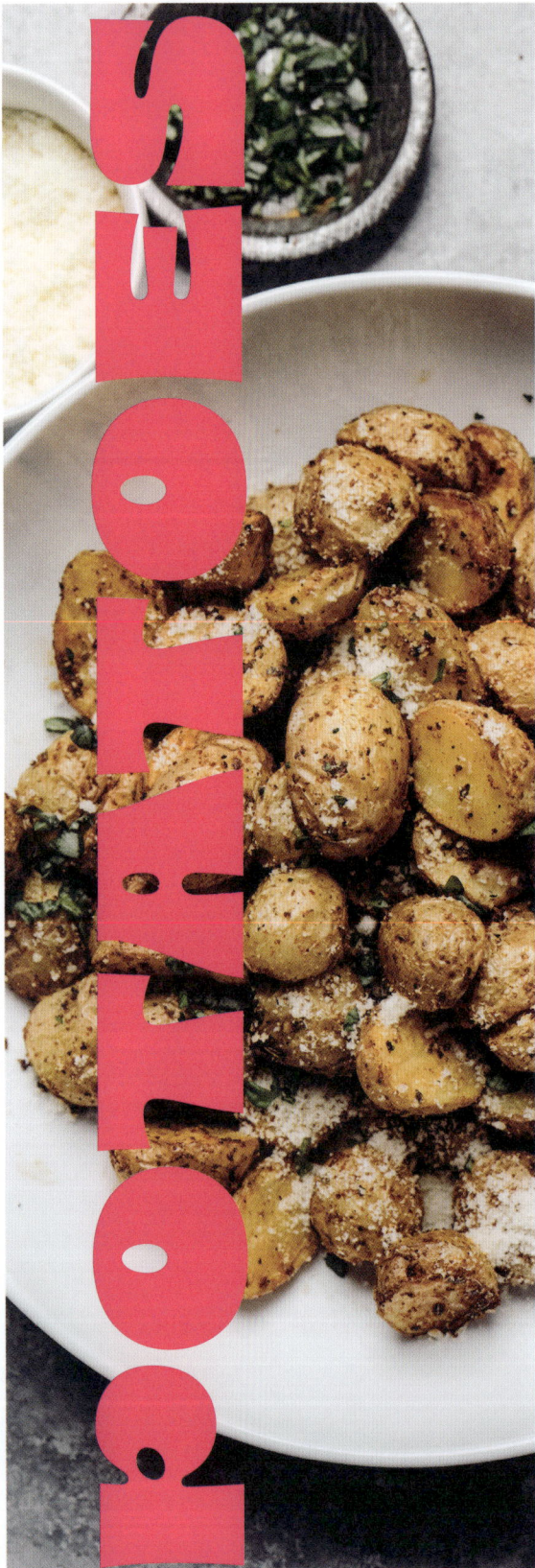

Healthy Mashed Potato

£ **Veggie** **>20**

SERVES 2

500 g (1 lb) floury potatoes
50 ml (2 fl oz) half-fat crème fraîche
salt and pepper

Cut the potatoes into chunks and cook in a large saucepan of lightly salted, boiling water for 15–20 minutes until tender. Drain, reserving 2 tablespoons of the cooking water and return the potatoes to the saucepan with the water.

Mash well until smooth. Stir in the crème fraîche and plenty of pepper, then serve.

TIP
Mix and match any of the following ingredients, adding when mashing: finely grated zest of 1 lemon; a handful of finely chopped herbs such as dill, parsley, chervil, tarragon or chives; 2 tablespoons chopped, drained capers or a small garlic clove, finely crushed. You can also use 3–4 tablespoons olive oil or milk instead of the crème fraîche, or swap half of the potatoes for the same weight of parsnips, celeriac or carrots, cooking them in the same pan as the potatoes.

Perfect
Roast Potatoes

££ **Vegan**

>50

SERVES 4–6

1kg (2 lb) floury potatoes
3 tablespoons olive oil
sea salt

Peel and cut potatoes into even-sized pieces. Parboil in a saucepan of lightly salted boiling water for 10 minutes, then drain well. Shake them after draining to rough up the edges slightly.

Pour the oil into a large roasting tin and heat in a preheated oven, 220°C (425°F), Gas Mark 7, for about 5 minutes or until the oil is very hot. Carefully place the potatoes in it, turning them over in the oil and then lightly sprinkle with sea salt.

Roast on the top shelf in the oven for 40 minutes, turning every now and then, until golden and crispy. Serve immediately.

Roasted Leeks
& Potatoes

£ **Vegan**

>20

SERVES 4

1 kg (2 lb) floury potatoes, peeled and cut into
2.5 cm (1 inch) cubes
2 leeks, trimmed, cleaned and thickly sliced
3 tablespoons olive oil
salt and pepper

Toss the potatoes and leeks with the oil on a large baking tray and season well. Roast in a preheated oven, 170°C (340°F), Gas Mark 3, for 30–40 minutes until golden and soft.

Enjoy hot or store in an airtight container in the refrigerator for up to 5 days.

TIP
Two of the cheapest vegetables out there, these deceptively simple flavours are the perfect base for so many things. If you'd rather not roast the leeks and potatoes, you can cook them in a frying pan instead.

Baked Potatoes

MAKES 8

8 large baking potatoes, such as Maris Piper or King Edward
a little flavourless oil (optional)
salt (optional)

Prick the potatoes all over with a knife or fork. If you like your potatoes to have a crunchy exterior, rub them all over with oil, then sprinkle with salt.

Bake in a preheated oven, 180°C (350°F), Gas Mark 4, for 1–2 hours, depending on size, until tender all over when gently squeezed. If you're in a hurry, try microwaving the potatoes for 7–8 minutes, then finishing them off in the oven for 15 minutes instead.

TIP
Bake at least 4 potatoes at a time to save on fuel costs and keep them in the refrigerator ready to make into loaded baked potatoes (see below).

Loaded Indian Potatoes

SERVES 2

2 large potatoes, baked (see above)
200 g (7 oz) frozen peas, defrosted
2 teaspoons garam masala, chaat masala or curry powder, plus extra to serve
large handful of coriander, finely chopped
½ red onion, finely chopped
1 tomato, finely chopped
¼ cucumber, finely chopped

LIMEY CASHEW CREAM

100 g (3½ oz) unsalted cashew nuts, soaked in cold water overnight or soaked in boiling water for 1 hour
4 tablespoons lime juice
salt and pepper

TIP
A fancy way to enjoy a baked potato, with a subtle warmth and a crunchy kachumber-style cucumber salad on top.

Make the limey cashew cream: drain and rinse the soaked cashews, then blitz in a food processor with 3 tablespoons of lime juice and a few splashes of water until you have a smooth, creamy sauce. Season to taste and set aside.

Split the potatoes in half, keeping them attached at the base. Scoop out the majority of the potato inside and transfer to a bowl. Add the peas and garam masala, chaat masala or curry powder and most of the coriander, saving some to serve. Season with salt and pepper, then spoon the mixture back into the potato skins and bake in a preheated oven, 180°C (350°F), Gas Mark 4, for 10–15 minutes until piping hot.

Meanwhile, mix the red onion, tomato and cucumber with the remaining lime juice and season with salt and pepper.

Spoon the limey cashew cream on top of the baked potatoes followed by the crunchy vegetable salad. Sprinkle with the remaining coriander and a little garam masala to serve.

Potato Wedges with Yogurt & Parsley Dip

£ | Veggie | <20

SERVES 1

1 potato, about 175 g (6 oz)
1 red pepper, cored, deseeded and sliced
1 teaspoon olive oil
paprika, to taste
salt and pepper

YOGURT AND PARSLEY DIP

3 tablespoons natural yogurt
1 tablespoon chopped parsley
2 spring onions, chopped
1 garlic clove, crushed (optional)

Cut the potato into 8 wedges and cook them in a saucepan of lightly salted boiling water for 5 minutes. Drain the wedges thoroughly, then put them into a bowl with the red pepper slices and toss with the oil. Sprinkle with paprika and salt to taste.

Arrange the potato wedges and pepper slices on a baking tray and cook under a preheated hot grill for 6–8 minutes, turning occasionally, until cooked.

Meanwhile, for the yogurt and parsley dip, put the yogurt, parsley, spring onions and garlic, if using, into a bowl. Season to taste with salt and pepper and mix thoroughly.

Serve the potato wedges and pepper slices hot with the yogurt dip.

Sweet Potatoes with Tomato Salsa

£ | Veggie | >50

SERVES 4

4 large sweet potatoes, about 275 g (9 oz) each
2 tablespoons olive oil
100 g (3½ oz) Emmental or Cheddar cheese, grated
salt

TOMATO SALSA

4 large tomatoes
1 small red onion, finely chopped
2 celery sticks, finely chopped
handful of coriander, chopped
4 tablespoons lime juice
4 teaspoons caster sugar

Scrub the potatoes and place in a small roasting tin. Prick with a fork, drizzle with the oil and sprinkle with a little salt. Put in a preheated oven, 200°C (400°F), Gas Mark 6, for 45 minutes until tender.

Meanwhile, make the salsa. Finely chop the tomatoes and mix with the onion, celery, coriander, lime juice and sugar in a bowl.

Halve the potatoes and fluff up the flesh with a fork. Sprinkle with the cheese and top with the salsa.

TIP

There are plenty of easy toppings for the humble but healthy sweet potato. Try feta and olives, tinned tuna mixed with natural yogurt or steamed broccoli and Cheddar.

Light Egg-Fried Rice

£ · Veggie · <20

SERVES 4

4 eggs
2 teaspoons peeled and finely chopped fresh
    root ginger
1½ tablespoons light soy sauce
2 tablespoons groundnut oil
300 g (10 oz) freshly cooked jasmine rice or long-
    grain rice, cooled
2 spring onions, thinly sliced
¼ teaspoon sesame oil

Beat the eggs with the ginger and half of the soy sauce in a bowl until combined.

Heat the groundnut oil in a nonstick wok or large frying pan over a high heat until the oil starts to shimmer. Pour in the egg mixture and cook, stirring constantly, for 30 seconds or until softly scrambled.

Add the cooked rice, spring onions, sesame oil and remaining soy sauce to the pan and toss together for about 1–2 minutes until the rice is piping hot. Serve immediately.

VARIATION

For **fried rice with Chinese leaves and chilli**, follow the recipe above, adding 1 deseeded and sliced red chilli and 125 g (4 oz) shredded Chinese leaves once the rice is piping hot, tossing together for a further 30 seconds.

Stir-Fried Veg Rice

£ · Veggie · <20

SERVES 4

2 tablespoons sunflower oil
6 spring onions, cut diagonally into 2.5 cm (1 inch)
    lengths
2 garlic cloves, crushed
1 teaspoon peeled and finely grated fresh
    root ginger
1 red pepper, cored, deseeded and finely chopped
1 carrot, finely diced
300 g (10 oz) peas
500 g (1 lb) ready-cooked long-grain rice
1 tablespoon dark soy sauce
1 tablespoon sweet chilli sauce

TO GARNISH

chopped coriander
chopped mint

Heat the oil in a large nonstick wok. Add the spring onions, garlic and ginger and stir-fry over a high heat for 4–5 minutes, then add the red pepper, carrot and peas and stir-fry for 3–4 minutes.

Stir in the rice and soy and sweet chilli sauces and stir-fry for 3–4 minutes until the rice is heated through and piping hot. Remove from the heat and serve immediately, garnished with the chopped herbs.

Vegetable Pilau Rice

SERVES 8

2 tablespoons flavourless oil
2 onions, finely chopped
400 g (13 oz) mushrooms, roughly chopped
4 garlic cloves, finely chopped
300 g (10 oz) basmati rice, washed thoroughly
1 teaspoon salt
1 tablespoon ground turmeric
400 ml (14 fl oz) vegan stock
200 g (7 oz) frozen peas
large handful of coriander, roughly chopped,
  to serve

Heat the oil in a large saucepan over a medium heat. Fry the onions for 8–10 minutes until soft and translucent.

Add the mushrooms and cook for 5–6 minutes until golden; they may give off some moisture, so keep going to drive that off and cook them until they are starting to brown. Now tip in the garlic and cook for a final 2 minutes.

Pour in the rice, salt and turmeric and stir for 2–3 minutes to toast the rice.

Slowly add the stock, then place a tea towel on top of the pot, followed by a lid, lifting the corners of the towel up and over the lid to keep them away from the flames. Reduce the heat to as low as it will go and cook for 15 minutes.

After 15 minutes, tip the peas on top of the rice, replace the tea towel and lid and cook for a final 5 minutes.

Turn off the heat and leave to stand for 5 minutes before serving. Fluff up the rice with a fork, evenly distributing the peas as you do so. Serve with a scattering of coriander.

TIP
Serve this with curry or roasted vegetables. It's also fantastic refried in a pan with some oil for a quick fried rice dish.

On-the-Go Granola Bars

££ | Veggie | >20

MAKES 9

75 g (3 oz) butter, plus extra for greasing
75 ml (3 fl oz) honey
½ teaspoon ground cinnamon
100 g (3½ oz) ready-to-eat dried apricots, roughly chopped
50 g (2 oz) ready-to-eat dried papaya or mango, roughly chopped
50 g (2 oz) raisins
4 tablespoons mixed seeds, such as pumpkin, sesame and sunflower
50 g (2 oz) pecan nuts, roughly broken
150 g (5 oz) porridge oats

Grease a shallow 20 cm (8 inch) square tin.

Place the butter and honey in a saucepan and bring gently to the boil, stirring continuously, until the mixture bubbles. Add the cinnamon, dried fruit, seeds and nuts, then stir and heat for 1 minute.

Remove from the heat and add the oats. Stir well, then transfer to the prepared tin and press down well. Bake in a preheated oven, 190°C (375°F), Gas Mark 5, for 15 minutes until the top is just beginning to brown.

Leave to cool in the tin, then cut into 9 squares or bars to serve. Store in an airtight tin for up to 2 days.

BARS

Choc Cornflake Bars

£ · Veggie · <20

MAKES 12

50 g (2 oz) butter, plus extra for greasing
200 g (7 oz) milk chocolate, broken into pieces
2 tablespoons golden syrup
125 g (4 oz) cornflakes

Grease a 28 x 18 cm (11 x 7 inch) tin.

Melt the chocolate with the golden syrup and butter in a bowl over a pan of simmering water.

Stir in the cornflakes and mix well together.

Turn the mixture into the prepared tin, chill until set, then cut into 12 bars.

VARIATION

For **muesli & apricot crunch cakes**, replace the cornflakes with 125 g (4 oz) muesli and 50 g (2 oz) chopped dried apricots. Combine with the chocolate mixture, spoon into 12 paper cake cases and chill until set.

Banana Blondies

££ · Vegan · >50

MAKES 12

200 g (7 oz) vegan spread, plus extra
  for greasing
125 g (4 oz) caster sugar
125 g (4 oz) dark brown sugar
3 ripe bananas, mashed with a fork, plus 1 firm
  banana (optional)
150 g (5 oz) smooth peanut butter
125 ml (4 fl oz) dairy-free milk
1 teaspoon apple cider vinegar
250 g (8 oz) self-raising flour
100 g (3½ oz) vegan dark or white chocolate,
  roughly chopped

Grease a 30 x 20 cm (12 x 8 inch) cake tin.

Cream the spread and both sugars together until paler and fluffy, using an electric whisk. Beat in the mashed bananas and peanut butter.

In a separate jug, combine the milk and vinegar, then add half to the mashed banana mixture, followed by half the flour and mix well until fully combined. Repeat with the remaining wet and dry ingredients, then scrape into the prepared tin.

Peel and slice the firm banana, if using, and arrange on top of the batter.

Bake in a preheated oven, 180°C (350°F), Gas Mark 4, for 30 minutes until golden on top and risen. A skewer inserted into the centre should only have a few moist crumbs sticking to it.

Allow to cool in the tin for 20 minutes before transferring to a wire rack to cool completely. Slice into 12 square blondies.

Store in an airtight container for up to 4 days.

Rocky Road Slices

MAKES 12

225 g (7½ oz) butter, plus extra for greasing
3 tablespoons golden syrup
50 g (2 oz) cocoa powder
125 g (4 oz) digestive biscuits, roughly crushed
200 g (7 oz) marshmallows, each cut into 4
75 g (3 oz) Maltesers, roughly crushed
200 g (7 oz) milk chocolate
200 g (7 oz) plain dark chocolate
4 tablespoons chocolate sprinkles

Grease a 25 x 18 cm (10 x 7 inch) tin.

Melt the butter with the golden syrup and cocoa powder in a bowl over a pan of simmering water. Stir in the biscuits, marshmallows and Maltesers.

Pour the biscuit mixture into the prepared tin and chill for 15 minutes.

Melt the milk and plain chocolate together in a bowl over a pan of simmering water. Remove from the heat. Pour the chocolate over the chilled mixture and scatter with chocolate sprinkles.

Chill for 20 minutes, then cut into slices or squares.

Fabulous Flapjacks

MAKES 6

175 g (6 oz) vegan spread, plus extra
  for greasing
80 g (3¼ oz) golden syrup
250 g (8 oz) rolled oats
100 g (3½ oz) light brown sugar
75 g (3 oz) raisins (optional)
pinch of salt

Grease a 25 x 20 cm (10 x 8 inch) baking tin with spread.

In a small saucepan, melt together the spread and golden syrup.

Put the oats, sugar and raisins, if using, in a large bowl. Pour in the melted spread and syrup, stir well to combine and add the pinch of salt.

Push the oat mixture into the prepared tin, using your hands to press it down evenly. Score the flapjack into 6 rectangles to help you to cut it after it's baked.

Bake in a preheated oven, 160°C (325°F), Gas Mark 3, for 25–30 minutes until golden. Allow to cool in the tin for at least 1 hour, then slice and store in an airtight container for up to 4 days.

TIP

Customize these flapjacks with whatever you want – try adding any dried nuts and fruit you like, or even chocolate chips.

Easy Almond Macaroons

SERVES 6

2 egg whites
100 g (3½ oz) golden caster sugar
100 g (3½ oz) ground almonds
blanched whole almonds, to decorate

TIP

For scribbled chocolate macaroons, make the macaroons as above, replacing 20 g (¾ oz) of the ground almonds with 20 g (¾ oz) cocoa powder and omitting the whole almonds. Heat 50 g (2 oz) plain dark or milk chocolate, evenly chopped, in a microwave-proof mug in a microwave in two or three 30-second bursts, stirring in between, until melted. Drizzle over the cooled biscuits with a teaspoon. Leave the chocolate to set before serving.

Line a large baking sheet with baking paper.

Whisk the egg whites in a clean bowl with a hand-held electric whisk until soft peaks form. Gradually whisk in the sugar, a spoonful at a time, until thick and glossy. Fold in the ground almonds until combined.

Drop dessert spoonfuls of the mixture, slightly apart, on to the prepared baking sheet. Press an almond on top of each.

Bake in a preheated oven, 180°C (350°F), Gas Mark 4, for about 15 minutes until the biscuits are pale golden and just crisp. Leave on the paper to cool for 5 minutes, then transfer to a wire rack to cool completely before serving.

Sultana & Ginger Cupcakes

MAKES 12

50 g (2 oz) piece of fresh root ginger
125 g (4 oz) lightly salted butter, softened
125 g (4 oz) caster sugar
2 eggs
150 g (5 oz) self-raising flour
½ teaspoon baking powder
½ teaspoon vanilla extract
50 g (2 oz) sultanas
200 g (7 oz) icing sugar
several pieces of crystallized ginger, very thinly sliced, to decorate

Line a 12-section muffin tray with paper cake cases.

Peel and finely grate the ginger, working over a plate to catch the juice. Put the butter, caster sugar, eggs, flour, baking powder and vanilla extract in a bowl. Add the grated ginger, reserving the juice for the icing. Beat with a hand-held electric whisk for about a minute until light and creamy.

Stir in the sultanas and then divide the cake mixture between the paper cases.

Bake in a preheated oven, 180°C (350°F), Gas Mark 4, for 20 minutes or until risen and just firm to the touch. Transfer to a wire rack to cool.

Beat the icing sugar in a bowl with the ginger juice, making up with enough water to create an icing that just holds its shape. Spread over the tops of the cakes with a small palette knife. Decorate with the crystallized ginger slices.

Any Berry Muffins

£ Vegan >20

MAKES 12

75 ml (3 fl oz) flavourless oil, plus extra for greasing (optional)
250 ml (8 fl oz) dairy-free milk
1 teaspoon apple cider vinegar or white wine vinegar
1 teaspoon vanilla extract (optional)
150 g (5 oz) caster sugar or light brown sugar
350 g (11½ oz) self-raising flour
1 teaspoon bicarbonate of soda
1 teaspoon fine sea salt
250 g (8 oz) berries (strawberries, raspberries, blueberries or blackberries, or a mixture of these)
3 tablespoons demerara sugar, for sprinkling (optional)

Line a muffin tray with 12 muffin cases. If you don't have cases, you can simply grease the muffin tray, or use squares of baking paper pressed in as liners.

Put the wet ingredients in a small bowl and whisk well to combine.

In a large bowl, mix the sugar, flour, bicarbonate of soda and salt. Gradually add the wet ingredients to the bowl, whisking well to combine, until you have a smooth batter.

Fold in the berries, then divide the batter evenly between the muffin cases. Sprinkle with demerara sugar, if using, then bake in a preheated oven, 180°C (350°F), Gas Mark 4, for 14–16 minutes until well risen and golden brown. A skewer inserted into a muffin should come out with no wet batter stuck to it.

Leave to cool on a wire rack, then store in an airtight container.

TIP

These are great for using up any odds and ends of fruit punnets that you have left lying around. Try adding a pinch of ground cinnamon, or the finely grated zest of a lemon, for an extra hit of flavour. These muffins keep in an airtight container for up to 7 days and are the perfect portable breakfast.

Chocolate Sea Salt Cupcakes

MAKES 12

CUPCAKES

100 g (3½ oz) self-raising flour
100 g (3½ oz) light brown sugar
25 g (1 oz) cocoa powder
pinch of salt
75 ml (3 fl oz) hot coffee or boiling water
60 ml (2½ fl oz) dairy-free milk
60 ml (2½ fl oz) flavourless oil
1 teaspoon vanilla extract (optional)

ICING (OPTIONAL)

50 g (2 oz) 70% cocoa vegan dark chocolate
50 g (2 oz) icing sugar
2 tablespoons dairy-free milk
sea salt flakes, to sprinkle (optional)

Line a 12-hole cupcake tin or muffin tin with small cake cases, or just use squares of nonstick baking paper.

In a large bowl, whisk together the flour, sugar, cocoa powder and salt until no lumps remain.

Add the coffee or boiling water, milk, oil and vanilla extract, if using, and whisk well until you have a smooth batter.

Spoon 1–2 tablespoons of batter into each of the cake cases and bake in a preheated oven, 180°C (350°F), Gas Mark 4, for 14–16 minutes until firm and springy to the touch and a skewer inserted into the centre comes out clean.

Remove the cakes from the tin and leave to cool on a wire rack.

Once cool, if you are making the icing, melt the chocolate in a microwave in 30-second bursts or in a heatproof bowl over a pan of just-boiled water (don't let the bowl touch the water). Whisk the melted chocolate with the icing sugar and milk until you have a thick but spreadable icing. Top each cake with 1 teaspoon of icing and a pinch of sea salt flakes, if using.

Store in an airtight container for up to 4 days.

TIP

If you don't have sea salt flakes, just add a pinch of regular salt to the chocolate icing. The coffee in the recipe brings out the chocolate flavour, but if you're not a coffee drinker just use hot water instead.

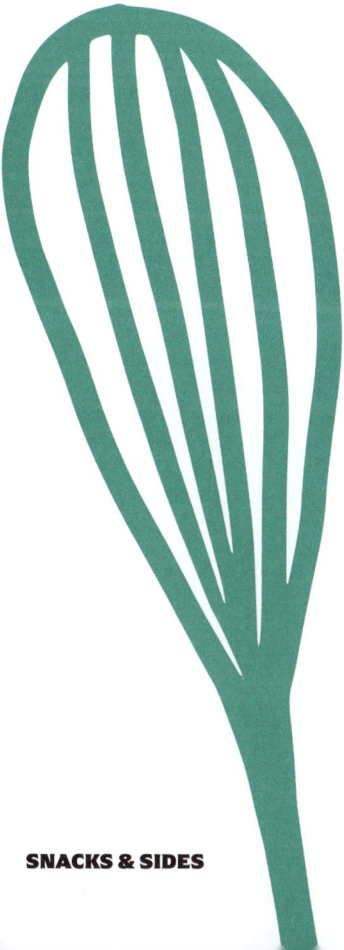

Peanut Butter Millionaire's 'Shortbread'

MAKES 9

'SHORTBREAD'

50 g (2 oz) rolled oats
50 g (2 oz) ground almonds
2 tablespoons golden syrup or maple syrup
20 g (¾ oz) vegan spread

TOPPING

20 g (¾ oz) unsalted peanuts
50 g (2 oz) coconut oil, melted
2 tablespoons golden syrup or maple syrup
175 g (6 oz) smooth peanut butter
100 g (3½ oz) 70% cocoa vegan dark chocolate
sea salt flakes (optional, see tip)

££

Vegan

>50

Line a 20 x 20 cm (8 x 8 inch) cake tin with baking paper in 2 strips, overlapping in a '+' shape.

Put the oats in a dry frying pan and place over a medium-high heat. Cook, stirring constantly, until they turn a shade darker and smell toasted. Tip into a bowl. Repeat with the ground almonds, then tip them into the bowl with the oats. Finally, toast the unsalted peanuts for the topping in the same way, then roughly chop them.

To make the 'shortbread', melt together the syrup and spread in a small saucepan. Add the toasted oats and ground almonds and stir well to combine. Press this mixture evenly into the prepared tin and refrigerate while you complete the next stage.

For the topping, whisk together the melted coconut oil, syrup and peanut butter. Pour over the prepared base and allow to set in the refrigerator for 1 hour.

Melt the chocolate in a microwave in 30-second bursts or in a heatproof bowl over a pan of just-boiled water (don't let the bowl touch the water).

Pour the chocolate over the peanut butter layer, smoothing out with the back of a spoon to get it into all the corners. Top with the chopped toasted peanuts and a sprinkle of sea salt flakes, if using.

Refrigerate until the chocolate has set, then cut into 9 squares with a sharp knife. Store in the refrigerator.

TIP
This take on the classic slice is rich, on a budget. If you can't stretch to sea salt flakes, then just add a pinch of regular salt to the peanut butter filling instead, or coarsely grind some cheaper rock salt and sprinkle it on top in place of the sea salt flakes. This is best served from the refrigerator, where it will stay perfectly fudgy for up to 5 days.

Choc Chip Cookies

££   Veggie   >20

MAKES 16
125 g (4 oz) unsalted butter, softened
175 g (6 oz) soft light brown sugar
1 teaspoon vanilla extract
1 egg, lightly beaten
1 tablespoon milk
200 g (7 oz) plain flour
1 teaspoon baking powder
250 g (8 oz) plain dark chocolate chips

Beat together the butter and sugar in a large bowl until pale and fluffy. Add the vanilla, then gradually beat in the egg, beating well after each addition. Stir in the milk. Sift in the flour and baking powder, then fold in. Stir in the chocolate chips.

Drop level tablespoonfuls of the mixture, about 3.5 cm (1½ inches) apart, on a large baking sheet lined with baking paper; lightly press with a floured fork. Bake in a preheated oven, 180°C (350°F), Gas Mark 4, for 15 minutes or until lightly golden. Transfer to a wire rack to cool.

Canned Fruit Tartlets

MAKES 6

plain flour, for dusting
320 g (11 oz) ready-rolled sheet vegan puff pastry
400 g (13 oz) can peach slices, syrup drained and reserved
finely grated zest and juice of 1 lemon
100 g (3½ oz) icing sugar

Roll out the pastry a little more on a lightly floured work top, trying to keep it in a rectangular shape. Cut the pastry into 6 evenly-sized rectangles and place on a large baking tray.

Arrange 4–5 peach slices on each pastry rectangle in a fan pattern, then brush with some of the syrup from the can and sprinkle with lemon zest.

Bake in a preheated oven, 180°C (350°F), Gas Mark 4, for 12–15 minutes until the pastry is puffed and golden brown.

Meanwhile, gradually add the juice of the lemon to the icing sugar until you have a thin icing of a pourable consistency.

Once cooked, allow the pastries to cool on the tray for 10 minutes before transferring to a wire rack. Drizzle each tartlet with icing and allow to set before serving.

TIP

Having a stash of canned fruit and some vegan puff pastry in the refrigerator or freezer means you can whip up an economical, fuss-free pudding in no time. Swap the peaches here for apricots or mango, if you prefer.

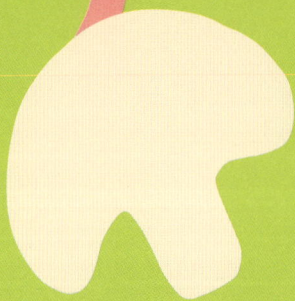

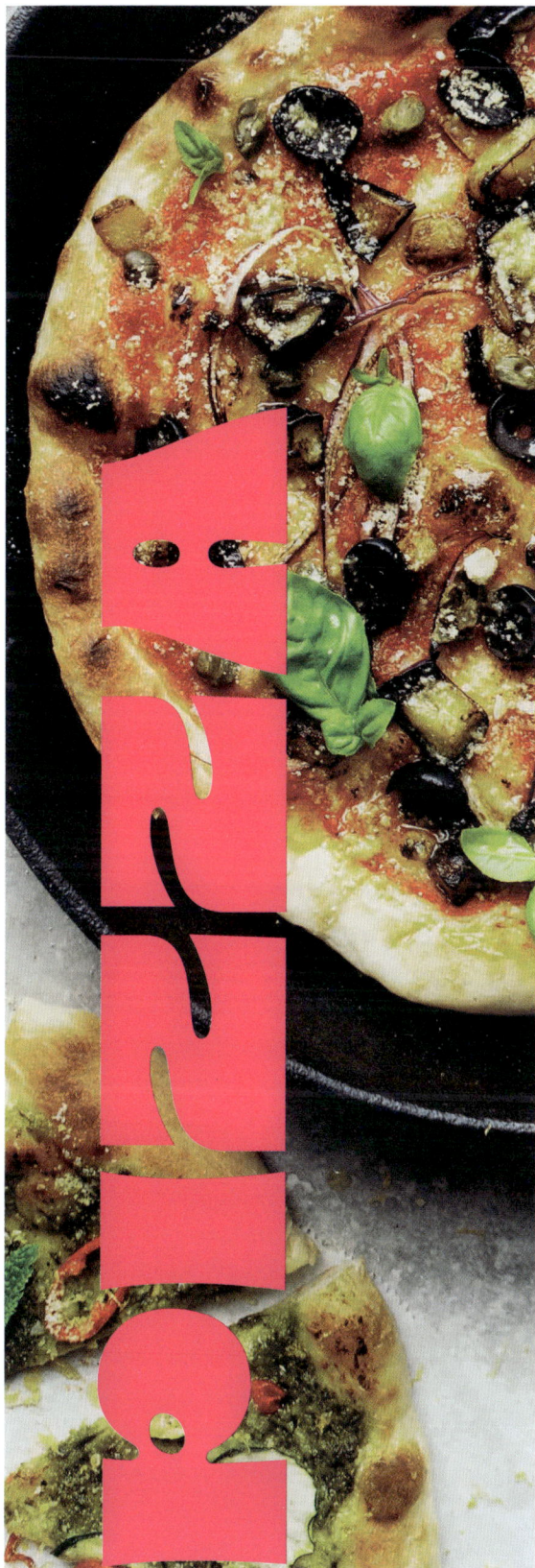

Pizza Caponata

££   **Vegan**   **>50**

SERVES 3–4

3 tablespoons olive oil, plus extra for drizzling
1 small aubergine, cut into small cubes
1 quantity Homemade Pizza Dough (see page 201)
1 quantity Marinara Sauce (see page 105)
15–20 black or green olives, halved
3–4 tablespoons drained capers
½ red onion, finely sliced
small handful of basil leaves (optional)
Vegan Parmesan (see page 214, optional)

Heat the olive oil in a large frying pan and fry the aubergine until tender and golden brown.

Make the pizza dough (see page 201). Top each pizza base with a few tablespoons of marinara sauce, a handful of aubergine pieces, 5 olives, 1 tablespoon of capers and a few red onion slices.

Cook the pizzas as instructed on page 201. Enjoy hot with a drizzle of olive oil, with some basil and vegan parmesan, if you like.

TIP
Sharp and sweet, caponata deserves to be much more than a dip. Think of this as the vegan equivalent of an anchovy and olive number.

Mushroom, Spinach & Garlic Pizza

>50

SERVES 3–4

100 g (3½ oz) unsalted cashew nuts, soaked in cold water overnight, or soaked in boiling water for 1 hour
3 tablespoons lemon juice
2 tablespoons extra virgin olive oil or regular olive oil, plus extra for drizzling
300 g (10 oz) mushrooms, finely sliced
200 g (7 oz) spinach
1 quantity Homemade Pizza Dough (see page 201)
2 garlic cloves, finely sliced
Vegan Parmesan (see page 214, optional)
salt and pepper

TIP

The cashew cream base in this recipe mimics a traditional white-based pizza bianca, which has no tomato sauce. Don't be afraid to add lots of lemon juice: it is needed to bring the toppings to life.

Drain and rinse the soaked cashews and blitz in a food processor with the lemon juice and a few splashes of water until you have a very smooth and creamy sauce, just thicker than double cream. Season to taste.

Heat the olive oil in a large frying pan and fry the mushrooms until tender and golden brown (this will take 5–6 minutes). Turn off the heat, add the spinach to the pan and allow to wilt.

Make the pizza dough (see page 201). Top each pizza base with a few tablespoons of cashew cream, followed by a large handful of mushrooms and spinach and some garlic slices.

Cook the pizzas as instructed on page 201. Enjoy hot with a drizzle of olive oil and vegan parmesan, if you like.

Frying Pan Pizza

>20

SERVES 4

300 g (10 oz) self-raising flour, plus extra for dusting
1 teaspoon dried thyme
150 ml (¼ pint) warm water
1½ tablespoons olive oil
6 tablespoons ready-made pizza or tomato pasta sauce
50 g (2 oz) can anchovies, drained
2 tablespoons drained capers
125 g (4 oz) mozzarella cheese, diced
salt and pepper

Mix the flour in a bowl with the thyme and a generous pinch of salt and pepper. Pour in the warm water and olive oil, and mix to form a soft dough.

Divide the dough in half and roll out on a lightly floured surface to fit 2 large nonstick frying pans, approximately 28 cm (11 inches) across. Dust with a little flour. Heat the frying pans over a medium heat and lower the circles of dough carefully into the pans. Cook for about 10 minutes, turning once, until lightly golden.

Spread the sauce over the pizza bases and scatter with anchovies and capers. Sprinkle over the mozzarella and cook under a preheated grill for 3–5 minutes, until golden and bubbling. Serve immediately.

Pizza Marinara

SERVES 3–4

1 quantity Homemade Pizza Dough (see page 201)
1 garlic clove, finely sliced (optional)
15 cherry tomatoes, halved (optional)
pinch of dried oregano (optional)
extra virgin olive oil or regular olive oil,
  for drizzling

MARINARA SAUCE

400 g (13 oz) can whole plum tomatoes
½ garlic clove, grated
2 tablespoons tomato purée
salt and pepper

To make the marinara sauce, either squeeze the whole plum tomatoes in your hands to break them up or quickly whizz them in a food processor. Stir in the grated garlic and tomato purée and season generously with salt and pepper.

Make the pizza dough (see page 201). Top each pizza base with a fairly thin layer of marinara sauce – 2–3 tablespoons willl be enough. Sprinkle with a few slices of garlic, cherry tomato halves and a pinch of dried oregano, if you like.

Cook the pizzas as instructed on page 201. Enjoy hot with a drizzle of olive oil.

TIP

The simplest, cheapest way to top a pizza, this just happens to be one of the most delicious as well. You'll soon be a big fan of uncooked tomato sauce, as it tastes so fresh when it's flashed in the oven on the pizza base and requires minimal effort. If you have leftover sauce, use it with pasta.

Spiral Tart

SERVES 6

500 g (1 lb) block vegan shortcrust pastry
plain flour, for dusting
1–2 courgettes
1–2 sweet potatoes, peeled
1 aubergine
2 garlic cloves, crushed
2 tablespoons olive oil
1 quantity Breadcrumb Pesto (see page 208)
leaves from 3 thyme sprigs
1 tablespoon chilli flakes
salt and pepper

Roll out the shortcrust pastry on a lightly floured work top to 1.5 cm (¾ inch) thick and use it to line a 25 cm (10 inch) fluted tart tin. Prick the base with a fork. Line the pastry case with baking paper and fill with baking beans or raw rice or dried beans. Bake in a preheated oven, 180°C (350°F), Gas Mark 4, for 15 minutes, until the pastry is sandy to the touch with no uncooked patches. Remove the baking paper and cook for a further 5 minutes until lightly golden.

Meanwhile, trim the ends off the vegetables, slice them thinly, then cut into half-moon shapes. Toss the vegetables with the garlic and oil in a large bowl.

Spread the pesto over the base of the pastry case. To decorate, place a circle of aubergine half moons around the edge of the tart, then a circle of sweet potato, then a circle of courgette, alternating the vegetables until the base is filled, to create a flower-like pattern.

Sprinkle with thyme and chilli flakes, season well with salt and pepper, then bake for 40 minutes until the vegetables are tender and cooked through. Check after 20 minutes and cover the edges of the pastry with foil if they seem to be catching during the long cooking time.

TIP
This finely sliced vegetable tart is a total show-stopper and all it requires is a little bit of your time to decorate it.

Caramelized Shallot & Tomato Tart

SERVES 4–6

1 quantity Confit Tomatoes (see page 204)
6 shallots, finely sliced
1 teaspoon caster sugar
1 tablespoon red wine vinegar
200 g (7 oz) block vegan puff pastry
1 tablespoon dairy-free milk (optional)
3 tablespoons drained capers
finely grated zest of 1 lemon
leaves from 3 basil sprigs

Preheat the oven to 190°C (375°F), Gas Mark 5. Place a baking sheet or large baking tray in the oven to heat up.

Use 3 tablespoons of the oil from the Confit Tomatoes to fry the shallots in a large frying pan over a medium heat for 10 minutes until softened. Add the sugar and red wine vinegar and cook for a further 10 minutes until sticky and caramelized.

Roll the puff pastry out into a rectangle on a large sheet of baking paper and score a smaller rectangle 2.5 cm (1 inch) from the edge. Prick the inner rectangle with a fork, then cover with a layer of caramelized shallots.

Top evenly with the drained Confit Tomatoes. Brush the exposed edges of the pastry with the milk, if you like, slide the tart on its paper onto the preheated baking sheet or tray and bake for 25–30 minutes until the pastry is golden. Sprinkle the tart with the capers, lemon zest and basil leaves to serve.

TIP
You need to caramelize the shallots thoroughly here to unleash their flavour – it takes a while, but if you cook double you can use the leftovers in other tarts, in a quesadilla or use them as a base for a quick soup.

Spinach, Pea & Mint Filo Tart

SERVES 6

2 tablespoons olive oil, plus extra for brushing
300 g (10 oz) frozen peas, defrosted
300 g (10 oz) frozen spinach, defrosted and
   squeezed of all excess water
5 spring onions, finely sliced
1 quantity Pea & Mint Pesto (see page 214)
½ teaspoon freshly grated nutmeg
320 g (11 oz) packet vegan filo pastry sheets
leaves from 3 mint sprigs
finely grated zest of 1 lemon
salt and pepper

Heat the oil in a large frying pan and fry the peas, spinach and spring onions with a pinch of salt over a medium heat until no liquid remains in the pan and the spring onions are soft.

Turn off the heat and stir in the pesto, then season with nutmeg, salt and pepper.

Layer the filo sheets in a large deep baking tin, overlapping each sheet, and brushing each layer with olive oil, until the whole tin (and its sides) is lined with filo.

Spread the filling evenly across the middle, then scrunch up the overhanging pastry to form an edge.

Bake in a preheated oven, 200°C (400°F), Gas Mark 6, for 15 minutes until the filling is firm and the pastry is deep golden brown. Sprinkle with the mint leaves and lemon zest and serve.

Beetroot Tarte Tatin

SERVES 6

320 g (11 oz) block vegan puff pastry
2 tablespoons olive oil
2 red onions, finely sliced
1 tablespoon caster sugar
1 tablespoon balsamic vinegar
leaves from 2 thyme sprigs, plus extra to serve
400 g (13 oz) cooked beetroot, cut into wedges
salt and pepper

Roll out the pastry to 5 mm (¼ inch) thick. Use a dinner plate as large as the ovenproof frying pan in which you will cook the tarte, as a template to cut out a circle of pastry and place on some baking paper. Transfer this to a tray and keep in the refrigerator until you need it.

Heat the oil in the ovenproof frying pan and fry the red onions for 15 minutes over a low heat or until deeply caramelized. Sprinkle over the sugar, vinegar and thyme and stir well to combine. Add the beetroot wedges in a snug single layer in a concentric circle pattern. Turn off the heat.

Cover the onions and beetroot with the puff pastry circle, tucking the edges down the side of the pan.

Bake in a preheated oven, 200°C (400°F), Gas Mark 6, for 30 minutes until the pastry is golden and well risen. Remove from the oven and leave to stand for 10 minutes before inverting onto a large serving dish. Scatter with thyme leaves and season well with salt and pepper.

TIP

This uses vacuum-packed beetroot that are readily available in supermarkets (just make sure they're not pickled in vinegar).

Chicken Tacos & Hot Green Salsa

>20

SERVES 4

1 tablespoon sunflower oil
4 x 175 g (6 oz) boneless, skinless chicken breasts

FOR THE HOT GREEN SALSA

1 avocado, chopped
1 red onion, finely chopped
1–2 hot green or red chillies, finely chopped
1 garlic clove, finely chopped
1 bunch coriander, roughly chopped
4 tablespoons lime juice
4 tablespoons olive oil
salt and pepper

TO SERVE

16 taco shells
150 ml (¼ pint) soured cream

Brush the chicken breasts with sunflower oil, then place them in a preheated frying pan and cook for 8–10 minutes on each side. Remove from the pan and slice into strips.

To make the salsa, place the avocado in a bowl and add the onion, chillies, garlic and coriander. Mix together, adding the lime juice, olive oil and seasoning.

Pile some of the salsa in each of the taco shells and top with a few strips of chicken. Serve the remaining salsa separately, with a bowl of soured cream to spoon on top of the tacos just before eating.

Chilli Tacos

>20

SERVES 4

2 tablespoons olive oil
1 large onion, finely chopped
2 garlic cloves, crushed
500 g (1 lb) lean minced beef
700 g (1 lb 7 oz) tomato passata
400 g (13 oz) can red kidney beans, rinsed
   and drained
2–3 tablespoons hot chilli sauce
salt and pepper

TO SERVE

8 soft corn tortillas (see page 202)
125 g (4 oz) Cheddar cheese, grated
125 g (4 oz) soured cream
handful of coriander sprigs

Heat the oil in a saucepan, add the onion and garlic and cook over a high heat for 5 minutes until softened. Add the minced beef and cook for 5 minutes until browned, breaking it up with a wooden spoon.

Stir in the passata, beans, chilli sauce and salt and pepper to taste and bring to the boil. Reduce the heat and simmer for 15 minutes until it has thickened.

Meanwhile, put the tortillas on a large baking sheet and warm through in a preheated oven, 220°C (450°F), Gas Mark 8, for 3–5 minutes to soften.

Place the tortillas on a serving plate in the centre of the table. Take 2 tortillas per person and spoon some chilli into each one. Top with a quarter of the cheese and soured cream and a little coriander, roll up and serve.

Smoky Mushroom Taco Bowls

SERVES 6

3 tablespoons flavourless oil, plus extra for oiling
1 quantity Taco Night Tortillas (see page 202)
500 g (1 lb) chestnut mushrooms, finely sliced
2 garlic cloves, grated
2 teaspoons smoked paprika
2 tablespoons tomato purée
1 quantity Limey Cashew Cream (see page 153)

TO GARNISH

5 radishes, finely sliced
½ onion, finely chopped
coriander sprigs

TIP
Use any mushroom you can find to make these little taco bowls – oyster mushrooms are particularly good. The tacos are twice cooked so are a good way to use up any leftover tortillas.

Oil the underside of a muffin tray, place a tortilla around each mould, then bake in a preheated oven, 180°C (350°F), Gas Mark 4, for 10 minutes until crisp and holding their bowl shapes. Set aside.

Heat the oil in a large frying pan. Add the mushrooms and cook for 5–6 minutes until golden brown. Add the garlic and cook for a further minute, followed by the paprika and tomato purée. Add a splash of water and cook for a further 2 minutes.

Fill each taco bowl with a few tablespoons of smoky mushrooms and a dollop of limey cashew cream. Garnish with radishes, onion and coriander.

Chargrilled Corn & Pepper Tacos

SERVES 6

2 x 300 g (10 oz) cans sweetcorn, drained
2 red peppers, cored, deseeded and finely sliced
2 green peppers, cored, deseeded and finely sliced
1 tablespoon ground cumin
finely grated zest and juice of 1 lime
1 quantity Taco Night Tortillas (see page 202)
salt and pepper

TO SERVE

1 quantity Tomato Salsa (see page 211)
coriander sprigs

Heat a large dry frying pan over a high heat. Add the sweetcorn and peppers and cook for 6–7 minutes until charred and blistered. Take off the heat and sprinkle with the cumin, lime zest and juice. Season with salt and pepper.

Serve the vegetables in the tacos with tomato salsa and coriander.

Spinach & Potato Tortilla

£ | Veggie | >20

SERVES 4

3 tablespoons olive oil
2 onions, finely chopped
250 g (8 oz) cooked potatoes, peeled and cut into
  1 cm (½ inch) cubes
2 garlic cloves, finely chopped
200 g (7 oz) cooked spinach, drained thoroughly
  and roughly chopped
4 tablespoons finely chopped, drained, roasted
  red peppers (in oil, from a jar)
5 eggs
3–4 tablespoons grated Manchego-style cheese
salt and pepper

Heat the oil in a nonstick, ovenproof frying pan and add the onions and potatoes. Cook over a medium heat for 3–4 minutes or until the vegetables have softened but not coloured, turning and stirring often. Add the garlic, spinach and peppers and stir to mix well.

Beat the eggs lightly in a jug and season well with salt and pepper. Pour the eggs into the frying pan, shaking the pan so that the egg mixture is evenly spread. Cook gently for 8–10 minutes or until the tortilla is set at the bottom.

Sprinkle over the grated cheese. Place the frying pan under a preheated medium-hot grill and cook for 3–4 minutes or until the top is set and golden.

Remove from the heat, cut into 4 wedges and serve warm or at room temperature.

Butternut Squash & Ricotta Frittata

SERVES 8

1 tablespoon rapeseed oil
1 red onion, thinly sliced
450 g (14½ oz) peeled and deseeded butternut squash, diced
8 eggs
1 tablespoon chopped thyme
2 tablespoons chopped sage
125 g (4 oz) ricotta cheese
salt and pepper

Heat the oil in a large, deep, ovenproof frying pan over a medium-low heat, add the onion and butternut squash, then cover loosely and cook gently, stirring frequently, for 18–20 minutes or until softened and golden.

Lightly beat the eggs, thyme, sage and ricotta together in a jug, season well with salt and pepper and then pour evenly over the butternut squash. Cook for a further 2–3 minutes until the egg mixture is almost set, stirring occasionally with a heat-resistant rubber spatula to prevent the base from burning.

Slide the pan under a preheated medium-hot grill and grill for 3–4 minutes or until the top is set and the frittata is golden. Slice into 6 wedges and serve hot.

£   Vegan   <20

Carrot Lentil Fritters

SERVES 4

250 g (8 oz)/about 1 serving Home-Style Dhal (see page 132)
50 g (2 oz) gram (chickpea) flour
1 large carrot, peeled and grated
small handful of coriander, chopped
2 spring onions, finely sliced
finely grated zest and juice of 1 lime
flavourless oil, for deep-frying
salt and pepper

Mix the dhal with the gram flour, carrot, coriander and spring onions, then season with the lime zest and juice and some salt and pepper.

Heat 2.5 cm (1 inch) of oil in a large frying pan. When the oil shimmers, spoon in ladlefuls of the thick batter, and use the back of the ladle to spread each into a patty shape.

Cook for 3–4 minutes on each side until golden brown. Remove with a slotted spoon and drain on kitchen paper. Serve hot, while you cook the remaining fritters.

Back-of-the-Fridge Fritters

SERVES 3–4

FRITTERS

1–2 large baking potatoes, peeled and roughly chopped, or 2 portions of Mashed Potato (see page 84)
200 g (7 oz) frozen peas, defrosted
large handful of chives, finely chopped
large handful of coriander, finely chopped
2–3 spring onions, finely sliced
flavourless oil, for frying
salt and pepper

SWEETCORN SALSA

100 g (3½ oz) cherry tomatoes, roughly chopped
100 g (3½ oz) sweetcorn
1 green chilli, deseeded and finely sliced
1 spring onion, finely sliced
finely grated zest and juice of 1 lime
1 tablespoon olive oil

TIP

The perfect meal when all you have in the refrigerator are some old herbs and spring onions, and a few frozen peas in the freezer. (It's an extra bonus if you already have some leftover mashed potato.) You can add any leftover vegetables you have lying around, such as broccoli, greens or grated carrot, and the fritters also work really well with mashed sweet potato instead of regular potato. The tomato and sweetcorn salsa gives them a Mexican twist, but they're just as delicious on their own served with some hot sauce.

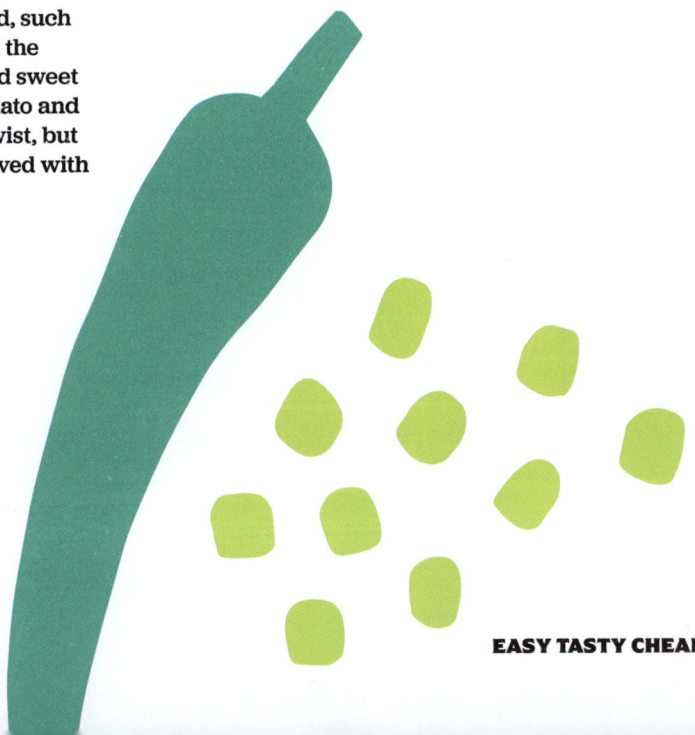

If you don't have any leftover mash, put the chopped potato into a pan of cold water and bring to the boil. Cook for 8–10 minutes until soft. Drain in a colander, then mash with a fork.

Add the peas, chopped herbs and spring onions and season well. Shape the mixture into 6–8 patties, depending how large you want them.

Heat 1 cm (½ inch) of oil in a large frying pan. Fry the potato fritters on each side for 3–4 minutes, in batches if you need to, so as not to crowd the pan. Try not to move them around too much – you want them to develop a crust and they can be quite delicate.

Meanwhile, mix all the ingredients for the salsa together in a small bowl.

Serve the fritters warm with the salsa on the side, making sure you get plenty of the limey tomato juice from the bottom of the bowl.

Spicy 'Tuna' Watermelon Tostadas

SERVES 6

1 small watermelon (about 1.25 kg/2½ lb), peeled
3 tablespoons soy sauce
finely grated zest and juice of 1 lime
2 tablespoons finely chopped pickled jalapeños
2 tablespoons sriracha or other hot sauce
flavourless oil, to deep-fry
1 quantity Taco Night Tortillas (see page 202)
salt

TO SERVE

1 quantity Avocado Crema (optional, see page 212)
shredded lettuce
spring onions, finely sliced
small handful of coriander, roughly chopped
1 lime, cut into wedges

Roast the watermelon on a large baking tray in a preheated oven, 200°C (400°F), Gas Mark 6, for 2 hours until shrunken slightly, charred and softened. Leave to cool, then slice, cube and transfer to a bowl with any roasting juices from the baking tray.

Add the soy sauce, lime zest and juice, pickled jalapeños and hot sauce to the bowl and leave to marinate for 1 hour.

Heat 1 cm (½ inch) of oil in a large frying pan. Fry the tortillas for 1 minute on each side until crisp and golden. Drain on kitchen paper and season with salt.

Top each tostada with the spicy watermelon cubes, avocado crema, if using, shredded lettuce, spring onions, coriander and lime wedges.

TIP
Roasting watermelon concentrates its flavour and lends it a firmer texture. Any leftovers of this spicy-sweet topping are also great served on a vegan poke bowl or just eaten with rice.

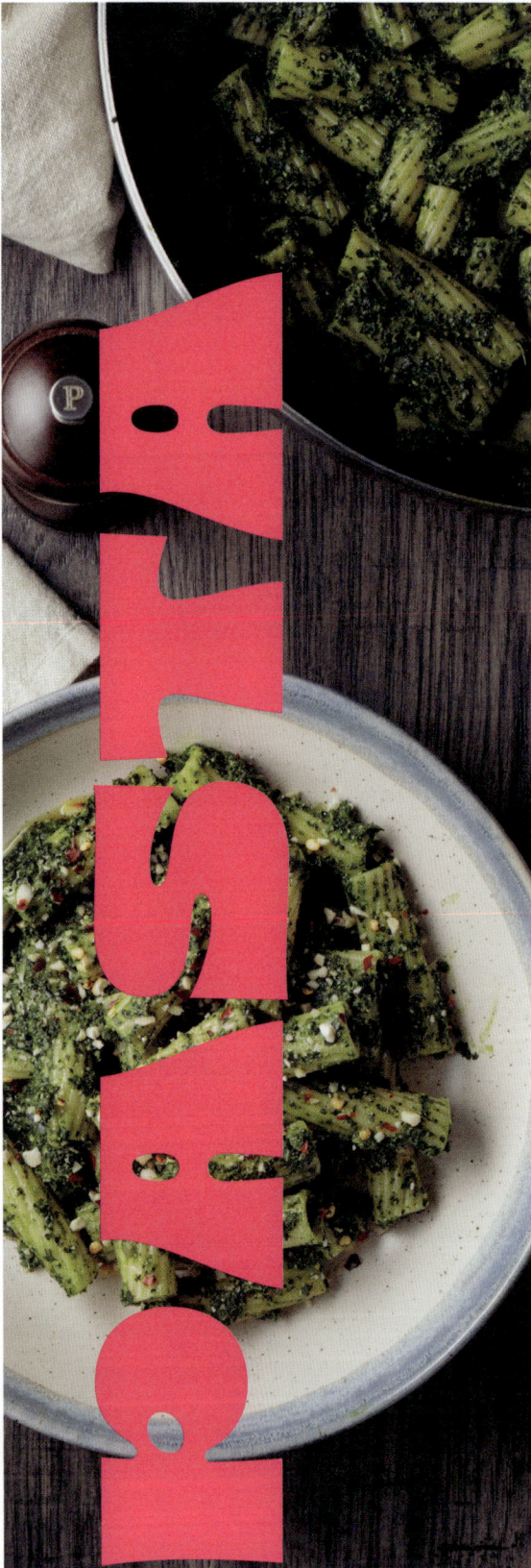

Pasta with Lentils, Kale & Onion

£ | Veggie | <20

SERVES 4

2 tablespoons olive oil
2 onions, cut into rings
pinch of dried chilli flakes
2 garlic cloves, finely sliced
50 g (2 oz) Puy lentils, rinsed and drained
400 g (13 oz) tricolore fusilli
125 g (4 oz) kale, chopped
salt and pepper

Heat the oil in a nonstick frying pan, add the onions and chilli flakes, season well and cook over a low heat for 15 minutes or until very soft and lightly browned. Add the garlic and cook for a further couple of minutes.

Meanwhile, cook the lentils in a saucepan of lightly salted simmering water according to the pack instructions, then drain.

While the onions and lentils are cooking, cook the pasta in a large saucepan of salted boiling water according to the pack instructions until al dente. Add the kale 3 minutes before the end of the cooking time and cook until tender. Drain, reserving a little of the cooking water, and return to the pan. Toss together with the lentils, adding a little cooking water to loosen if needed.

Spoon into bowls and scatter with the caramelized onions.

PASTA

££ Veggie

Aubergine Cannelloni

SERVES 4

4 sheets of fresh or dried lasagne, each about 18 x 15 cm (7 x 6 inches)
2 medium aubergines, thinly sliced
4 tablespoons olive oil
1 teaspoon finely chopped thyme
250 g (8 oz) ricotta cheese
25 g (1 oz) basil leaves, torn into pieces
2 garlic cloves, crushed
1 quantity Fresh Tomato Sauce (see page 203)
100 g (3½ oz) fontina or Gruyère cheese, grated
salt and pepper

Bring a saucepan of lightly salted water to the boil. Add the lasagne sheets, return to the boil and cook, allowing 2 minutes for fresh and 8–10 minutes for dried. Drain the sheets and immerse in cold water.

Place the aubergine slices in a single layer on a foil-lined grill rack. (You may need to do this in 2 batches.) Mix together the oil, thyme and some salt and pepper and brush over the aubergines. Grill under a preheated medium-hot grill until lightly browned all over, turning once.

Beat the ricotta in a bowl with the basil, garlic and a little salt and pepper. Thoroughly drain the pasta sheets and lay them on the work surface. Cut each one in half. Spread the ricotta mixture over the lasagne sheets, right to the edges. Arrange the aubergine slices on top. Roll up each pasta sheet to enclose the filling inside.

Spread two-thirds of the tomato sauce in a shallow ovenproof dish and arrange the cannelloni on top. Spoon over the remaining tomato sauce and then sprinkle with the cheese. Bake in a preheated oven, 190°C (375°F), Gas Mark 5, for 20 minutes or until the cheese is golden.

Mushroom & Cauliflower Bolognese

SERVES 8

3 tablespoons extra virgin olive oil or regular olive oil

750 g (1½ lb) chestnut mushrooms

1 cauliflower, leaves removed, broken into florets and stalk chopped

1 red onion, finely chopped

1 carrot, finely chopped (optional)

1 celery stick, finely chopped (optional)

3 garlic cloves, finely chopped

2 flat leaf parsley sprigs, roughly chopped, plus extra leaves to serve

100 ml (3½ fl oz) red wine

2 tablespoons tomato purée

400 g (13 oz) can chopped tomatoes or tomato passata

400 ml (14 fl oz) vegan stock

1 tablespoon balsamic vinegar or red wine vinegar

500 g (1 lb) spaghetti, cooked

salt and pepper

££

Vegan

>50

Heat the oil in a large casserole dish or large, deep saucepan. Blitz the mushrooms in a food processor until finely chopped – but be careful not to make them into a mushy purée – then transfer to the casserole dish or pan and cook over a medium-high heat until golden brown, about 5 minutes.

While the mushrooms cook, add the cauliflower to the food processor and pulse until the mixture resembles rice. Set aside.

Add the onion, carrot and celery, if using, to the mushroom mixture and cook for a further 8–10 minutes until everything is soft. Add the garlic and parsley sprigs and cook for 1 minute until fragrant.

Add the wine to the pan, if using, and let it bubble up and almost disappear, stirring with a wooden spoon to help deglaze any golden crust on the base of the pan.

Add the tomato purée, chopped tomatoes or passata and stock. Bring to the boil, then reduce the heat and simmer for 15–20 minutes until the sauce has reduced and thickened. Add the cauliflower and cook for a final 10 minutes.

Season with the vinegar, salt and pepper. Serve with cooked, drained spaghetti, with a little parsley sprinkled on top.

TIP

Deeply satisfying and with an incredible depth of flavour, this recipe works well with other vegetables too; swap the cauliflower for all mushrooms, or try adding lentils to bulk it out. The recipe works well without the carrot and celery, though they do add flavour, and you can leave out the red wine and simply add more water or stock.

Broccoli, Garlic, Lemon & Chilli Orecchiette

SERVES 6

1 large head of broccoli, broken into florets, stem roughly chopped

500 g (1 lb) orecchiette pasta

50 ml (2 fl oz) extra virgin olive oil or regular olive oil

4 garlic cloves, finely sliced

finely grated zest and juice of 1 lemon

2 teaspoons chilli flakes

3 tablespoons Vegan Parmesan (see page 214)

salt and pepper

TIP

This is a delicious broccoli sauce, but if you only have the garlic, chilli and lemon, that's also a banging budget supper.

Bring a large saucepan of salted water to the boil. Add the broccoli and blanch for 3 minutes until just tender. Transfer to a chopping board and allow the broccoli to cool briefly, then roughly chop it into smaller bite-sized pieces.

Cook the orecchiette.

Meanwhile, heat the oil in a large frying pan over a medium heat. Add the garlic and fry for 1–2 minutes until fragrant and lightly golden.

Add the cooked pasta to the frying pan with the broccoli. Season with the lemon zest and juice and add the chilli flakes. Toss everything together vigorously until the starch releases from the pasta to thicken the sauce, adding a splash of pasta water if necessary to loosen it. Serve with the Vegan Parmesan and a generous amount of pepper.

Spaghetti Carbonara

SERVES 4

400 g (13 oz) spaghetti

150 g (5 oz) streaky bacon

2 egg yolks

4 tablespoons double cream

25 g (1 oz) Parmesan cheese, grated, plus extra to serve

salt and pepper

Cook the pasta in a large saucepan of lightly salted boiling water according to the pack instructions until al dente.

Meanwhile, cook the bacon under a preheated medium grill for 7 minutes or until crisp. Cool for 1 minute, then cut into small pieces. Mix together the egg yolks, cream and Parmesan in a bowl.

Drain the pasta, reserving a little of the cooking water, and return to the pan. Stir in the bacon and cream mixture, adding a little cooking water to loosen if needed. Season well.

Pile on to plates, scatter with extra Parmesan.

Spinach & Butternut Lasagne

>50

SERVES 4

2 tablespoons olive oil
1 small butternut squash, about 700 g (1 lb 6 oz),
  deseeded, peeled and cut into small dice
1 teaspoon ground cumin
¼ teaspoon dried chilli flakes
400 g (13 oz) can chopped tomatoes
1 teaspoon caster sugar
200 g (7 oz) spinach
20 g (¾ oz) butter
2 tablespoons plain flour
300 ml (½ pint) semi-skimmed milk
100 g (3½ oz) mature Cheddar cheese, grated
100 g (3½ oz) dried lasagne sheets
salt and pepper
green salad, to serve

Heat the oil in a saucepan and gently fry the squash for 5 minutes, stirring. Add the cumin, chilli flakes, tomatoes and sugar and simmer gently, uncovered, for 20 minutes, stirring occasionally until the squash is tender. Stir in the spinach until wilted and season to taste with salt and pepper. Remove from the heat.

Melt the butter in a separate saucepan and stir in the flour, beating with a wooden spoon for 1 minute. Gradually stir in the milk and cook over a gentle heat, stirring continuously until thickened and smooth. Beat in half of the cheese and season to taste with salt and pepper. Remove from the heat.

Spread a quarter of the squash mixture into a shallow, ovenproof dish and cover with a layer of the lasagne sheets, breaking them to fit if necessary. Add another quarter of the squash mixture, spoon over about a third of the cheese sauce and cover with another layer of the lasagne sheets. Continue layering the ingredients in the same way, finishing with a layer of squash mixture topped with cheese sauce. Sprinkle with the remaining grated cheese.

Bake in a preheated oven, 190°C (375°F), Gas Mark 5, for 40 minutes until golden and bubbling. Serve with a green salad.

Spicy Green Bean, Potato & Pesto Linguini

>20

SERVES 4

200 g (7 oz) potatoes, peeled and cut into small
  cubes
200 g (7 oz) green beans, trimmed and halved
350 g (11½ oz) fresh linguini
2 red chillies, finely chopped
250 g (8 oz) shop-bought fresh green pesto
salt and pepper
grated pecorino cheese, to serve

Cook the potatoes in a large saucepan of lightly salted boiling water for 10–12 minutes until just tender, adding the beans and linguini 4 minutes before the end of the cooking time. Drain well, then return to the pan.

Mix together the chillies and pesto in a mug, then season well with salt and pepper. Spoon into the pasta mixture and toss to mix well. Divide among bowls and serve with grated pecorino cheese to sprinkle over.

Tuna Pasta Bake

>20

SERVES 4

300 g (10 oz) pasta shells
2 tablespoons olive oil
1 onion, finely chopped
2 red peppers, cored, deseeded and cubed
2 garlic cloves, crushed
200 g (7 oz) cherry tomatoes, halved
15 g (½ oz) butter
50 g (2 oz) fresh breadcrumbs
400 g (13 oz) can tuna, drained and flaked
125 g (4 oz) mozzarella cheese or Gruyère cheese, grated

Cook the pasta shells in a saucepan of lightly salted boiling water for 8–10 minutes, or according to the pack instructions, until al dente.

Meanwhile, heat the oil in a large frying pan. Add the onion and fry gently for 3 minutes. Add the peppers and garlic and carry on frying, stirring frequently, for 5 minutes. Stir in the tomatoes and fry for 1 minute until they are soft.

Melt the butter in another pan, toss in the breadcrumbs and stir until all the bread is covered in butter.

Drain the pasta, add the pepper and tomato mix, and then the tuna. Mix together, then put in an ovenproof dish.

Sprinkle the mozzarella or Gruyère and then the buttered breadcrumbs over the pasta and cook under a medium grill for 3–5 minutes until the cheese has melted and the breadcrumbs are golden.

Mac & Cheese with Spinach

££ **Veggie**

>20

SERVES 4

300 g (10 oz) macaroni
350 g (11½ oz) baby spinach leaves
50 g (2 oz) butter
50 g (2 oz) plain flour
750 ml (1¼ pints) milk
150 g (5 oz) Taleggio or fontina cheese, chopped
2 teaspoons wholegrain mustard
1 teaspoon Dijon mustard
8 cherry tomatoes, halved
50 g (2 oz) fresh white breadcrumbs
25 g (2 oz) Cheddar cheese, grated
salt and pepper

Cook the macaroni in a large saucepan of lightly salted boiling water for 8–10 minutes, or according to the packet instructions, until al dente.

Add the spinach to the pan and cook for 1 minute until wilted. Drain well and place in a 1.5 litre (2½ pint) ovenproof dish.

Meanwhile, place the butter, flour and milk in a saucepan and whisk constantly over a medium heat until the sauce boils and thickens. Simmer for 2–3 minutes until you have a smooth glossy sauce, then reduce the heat to low and stir in the Taleggio or fontina and mustards. Season to taste with salt and pepper and cook gently until the cheese has melted.

Pour the sauce over the macaroni and spinach, scatter over the tomatoes and then sprinkle with the breadcrumbs and Cheddar. Bake in a preheated oven, 200°C (400°F), Gas Mark 6, for 20 minutes until golden and bubbling.

Paella

SERVES 6

1 kg (2 lb) live mussels
4 garlic cloves
1 small bunch of mixed herbs
150 ml (¼ pint) dry white wine
2 litres (3½ pints) hot chicken stock (see page 197) or water
4 tablespoons olive oil
4 small cleaned squid, cut into rings
1 large onion, finely chopped
1 red pepper, cored, deseeded and chopped
4 large ripe tomatoes, skinned, deseeded and chopped
12 skinless, boneless chicken thighs, cut into bite-sized pieces
500 g (1 lb) paella rice
large pinch of saffron threads, crumbled
125 g (4 oz) fresh or frozen peas
12 large raw peeled prawns
salt and pepper

Scrub the mussels in cold water. Scrape off any barnacles and pull away the dark hairy beards. Discard any with damaged shells or open ones that do not close when tapped firmly with a knife. Set aside.

Slice 2 of the garlic cloves and crush the remainder. Place the sliced garlic in a large heavy-based saucepan with the herbs, wine and 150 ml (¼ pint) of the stock or water and season well with salt and pepper. Tip in the mussels, cover and cook, shaking the pan frequently, for 4–5 minutes until all the shells have opened. Lift out the mussels with a slotted spoon into a bowl, discarding any that remain closed. Strain the cooking liquid into a bowl and reserve.

Heat 2 tablespoons of the oil in the pan and fry the squid, stirring frequently, for 5 minutes. Add the onion, red pepper and crushed garlic and cook gently for 5 minutes, or until softened. Add the mussel cooking liquid and tomatoes and season with salt and pepper. Bring to the boil, then reduce the heat and cook gently, stirring, for 15–20 minutes until thickened. Transfer to a bowl.

Heat the remaining oil in the pan, add the chicken and fry for 5 minutes. Add the rice and cook, stirring, for 3 minutes.

Return the squid mixture to the pan, add one-third of the remaining stock and the saffron and bring to the boil, stirring. Cover and simmer, adding stock a little at a time, for 30 minutes, or until the chicken is cooked, the rice is tender and the liquid has been absorbed.

Taste and adjust the seasoning if needed. Add the peas and prawns and simmer, for 5 minutes, adding a little more stock if required. Return the mussels to the pan, cover and heat through for 5 minutes. Serve immediately.

Asparagus, Pea & Mint Risotto

££ **Veggie** **>50**

SERVES 4

500 g (1 lb) asparagus spears
1 litre (1¾ pints) vegetable stock (see page 197)
50 g (2 oz) butter
1 onion, finely chopped
300 g (10 oz) arborio, carnaroli or vialone
  nano rice
150 ml (¼ pint) dry white wine
100 g (3½ oz) shelled fresh or frozen peas
4 tablespoons freshly grated Parmesan-style
  cheese, plus extra to serve
handful of mint leaves, roughly chopped

Cut the asparagus in half, at an angle, separating the tips from the thicker stalks. Reserve the tips. Put the stalks in a saucepan with the stock and bring to the boil. Boil for 5 minutes, then reduce to a simmer. Remove the stalks with a slotted spoon and process to a purée in a food processor or blender. If you don't have a blender, mash the asparagus stalks well with a potato masher.

Melt half the butter in a heavy-based saucepan over a low heat. Add the onion and cook for 10 minutes until softened. Add the rice and cook, stirring, for 1 minute. Add the wine and cook, stirring, until absorbed. Stir in the puréed asparagus.

Add 2 ladlefuls of the simmering stock. Slowly simmer, stirring constantly, until the stock has been absorbed and the rice parts when a wooden spoon is run through it. Add another ladleful of stock and continue to cook, stirring and adding the stock in ladlefuls, reserving 2 ladlefuls, for 16–18 minutes until the rice is creamy and almost tender to the bite.

Add the peas and the reserved asparagus tips and stock and continue cooking until the stock is almost absorbed. Remove from the heat and stir in the cheese, mint and remaining butter. Stir vigorously for 15 seconds. Cover with a tight-fitting lid and leave to stand for 2 minutes. Serve immediately with extra cheese.

Bacon, Pea & Courgette Risotto

£

>20

SERVES 4

50 g (2 oz) butter
150 g (5 oz) streaky bacon, diced
300 g (10 oz) risotto rice
100 ml (3½ fl oz) dry white wine (optional)
900 ml (1½ pints) hot chicken or vegetable stock (see page 197) (add an extra 100 ml/3½ fl oz if not using wine)
2 courgettes, about 325 g (11 oz) in total, coarsely grated
200 g (7 oz) frozen peas, defrosted
1 small bunch of basil, shredded (optional)
salt and pepper
grated Parmesan cheese, to serve

Melt the butter in a large frying pan or saucepan and cook the bacon over a medium heat for 6–7 minutes until golden. Lift out half of the bacon with a slotted spoon on to a plate.

Add the rice to the pan and stir well. Pour in the wine, if using, and stock. Bring to the boil, then simmer gently for 15–18 minutes, stirring as often as possible, until the rice is tender and creamy. Stir in the courgette and peas for the final 2–3 minutes of the cooking time.

Season with salt and pepper, then spoon the risotto into 4 bowls. Scatter over the reserved bacon and the basil, if using. Serve sprinkled with grated Parmesan.

Pork & Tomato Rice Pot

££

>20

SERVES 4

3 tablespoons olive oil
300 g (10 oz) pork fillet, sliced
1 onion, finely chopped
3 garlic cloves, finely chopped
250 g (8 oz) paella rice
2 teaspoons smoked paprika
200 g (7 oz) can chopped tomatoes
650 ml (1 pint 2 fl oz) hot chicken stock (see page 197)
125 g (4 oz) baby spinach leaves
salt and pepper
lemon wedges, to serve

Heat 1 tablespoon of the oil in a large, deep frying pan over a high heat. Add the pork fillet and cook for 3 minutes until golden and nearly cooked through, then remove from the pan and set aside. Reduce the heat, add the onion to the pan with the remaining oil and cook for 3 minutes until softened, then stir in the garlic and cook for 30 seconds.

Add the rice and cook for 1 minute, then add the paprika and tomatoes, bring to the boil and simmer for 2–3 minutes. Pour in the stock, season to taste and cook for a further 12–15 minutes until there is just a little liquid left around the edges of the pan.

Lightly fork the spinach through the rice, arrange the pork on top, then cover and continue to cook for 3–4 minutes until cooked through. Serve with lemon wedges for squeezing over.

Budget Home-Style Dhal

£ • Vegan • >50

SERVES 6

1 tablespoon flavourless oil
2 onions, finely chopped
4 garlic cloves, crushed
large handful of coriander, stalks finely chopped, leaves reserved to garnish
20 g (¾ oz) fresh root ginger, peeled and grated
1 teaspoon ground turmeric
1 teaspoon garam masala
300 g (10 oz) red lentils, rinsed and drained
2 tomatoes or a handful of cherry tomatoes, roughly chopped
1 litre (1¾ pints) water or vegan stock
2 tablespoons lemon juice
salt and pepper

Heat the oil in a large saucepan. Add the onions and a pinch of salt and cook for 8–10 minutes until soft and translucent. Add the garlic, coriander stalks and ginger and cook for 2 minutes more.

Add the turmeric and garam masala and cook for 1 minute until fragrant.

Tip in the lentils and half the tomatoes. Stir to combine, then pour in the measured water or stock.

Bring to the boil, then reduce the heat and simmer for 25–30 minutes until the lentils are tender, stirring occasionally.

Season the dhal with the lemon juice and salt and pepper. Top with the remaining chopped tomato and the coriander leaves. This will keep in the refrigerator for up to 4 days and also freezes well.

TIP

If you're really struggling for cash you can leave out the ginger, coriander and tomatoes and it will still be just as delicious. Try adding coconut milk in place of the water – dhal is the perfect dish to experiment with.

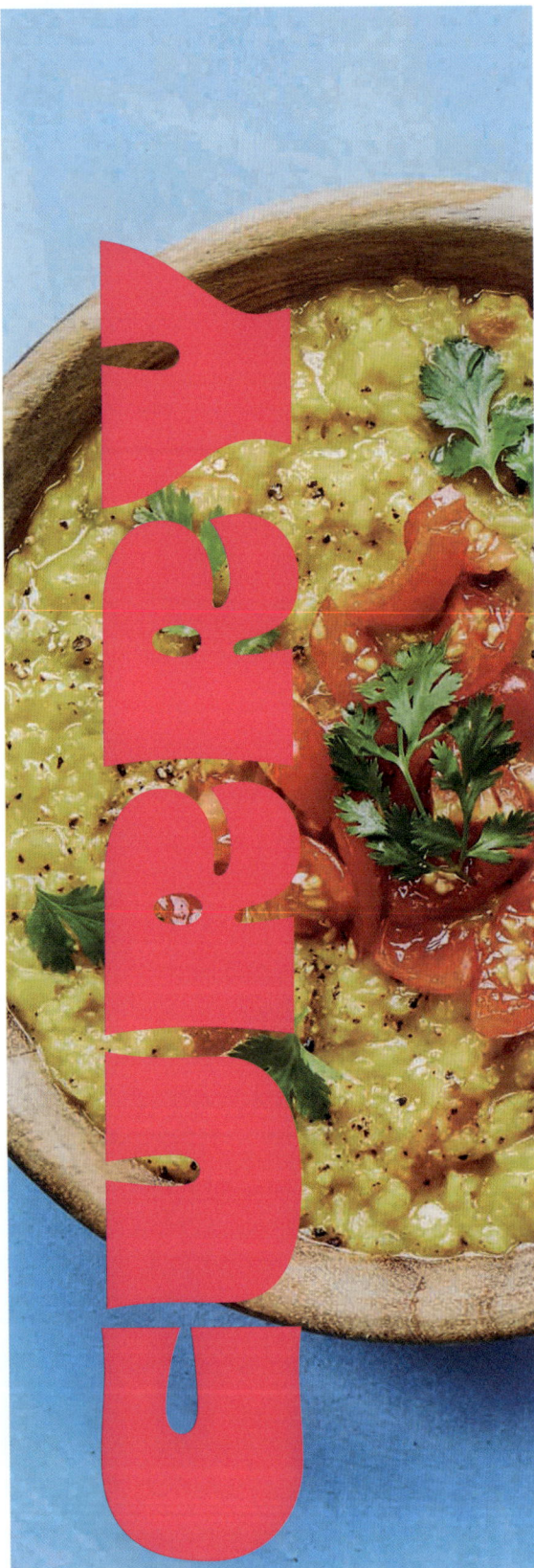

Chicken Curry in a Hurry

££   >20

SERVES 4

2 tablespoons sunflower oil
 4 skinless chicken thigh fillets, chopped
2 sweet potatoes, peeled and cubed
3 tablespoons balti curry paste
400 g (13 oz) can chopped tomatoes
300 ml (½ pint) chicken stock (see page 197)
125 g (4 oz) frozen peas
small handful of coriander leaves, roughly
   chopped
warm naan bread, to serve

Heat the oil in a large frying pan, add the chicken and sweet potatoes and fry, stirring, over a high heat for 5 minutes.

Add the curry paste, tomatoes and stock to the frying pan, bring to the boil, reduce the heat, cover and simmer for 10 minutes. Stir in the peas and cook for a further 5 minutes. Stir in the coriander and serve with warm naan bread.

TIP

Double up on the quantities of this quick curry and freeze half (before you add the coriander) for another meal.

Chicken Jalfrezi

££   >20

SERVES 2

2 tablespoons sunflower oil
300 g (10 oz) boneless, skinless chicken breasts,
   cut into pieces
1 onion, cut into thin wedges
1 small green pepper, cored, deseeded and cut
   into chunks
1 green chilli, deseeded and finely chopped
1 teaspoon ground cumin
1 teaspoon garam masala
1½ teaspoons ground turmeric
2 tomatoes, cut into wedges
2 tablespoons natural yogurt
200 ml (7 fl oz) hot water
warm naan bread, to serve

Heat the oil in a large frying pan, add the chicken, onion and green pepper and cook over a medium heat, stirring occasionally, for 10 minutes until chicken starts to turn golden. Add the chilli and spices and cook for 2–3 minutes, then stir in the tomatoes and cook for a further 3 minutes.

Stir in the yogurt, then pour in the measured hot water, cover and simmer very gently for 10 minutes until the chicken is cooked through and the flavours have infused, stirring occasionally and adding a little more water if necessary. Serve with warm naan bread to mop up the juices.

Sesame Aubergine Curry

SERVES 2

80 g (3¼ oz) raw peanuts

50 g (2 oz) sesame seeds

2 garlic cloves

large handful of coriander, stalks finely chopped, leaves reserved to garnish

2 tablespoons brown sugar

1 tablespoon curry powder

50 ml (2 fl oz) water, plus extra if needed

10 small aubergines, quartered, but left intact at the stalk end, or 2 regular aubergines, cut into small wedges

2 tablespoons flavourless oil

400 ml (14 fl oz) vegan stock

1 lime, cut into wedges, to garnish

salt and pepper

In a blender or a pestle and mortar, blitz or work together the peanuts, sesame seeds, garlic, coriander stalks, sugar and curry powder with the measured water, adding more to loosen if necessary – you want a spreadable paste.

Lay the aubergines on a large baking tray. Spoon the paste on to the cut sides of the aubergines (or, if using regular aubergines, just toss the wedges in the paste). If you have any curry paste left over, set it aside. Toss the aubergines in the oil and season well with salt and pepper.

Roast the aubergines in a preheated oven, 240°C (475°F), Gas Mark 9, for 5–8 minutes until starting to blister and sizzle. Add any remaining curry paste and the stock, stir briefly and cook for a further 10–12 minutes until the aubergine is tender and the sauce has reduced. Serve with lime wedges and coriander leaves.

TIP

This curry is quickest to prepare when you use baby aubergines, but you can use regular aubergines if you can't find them. It's a fairly dry curry using a quick nutty paste that you stuff inside the aubergines, which is cooked at a fiercely high heat to get it to your table in 20 minutes. It also works well as a slower-cooked dish if you prefer: cook it at 180°C (350°F), Gas Mark 4 for 35 minutes, covering with foil to prevent the liquid from evaporating. If you'd like it to be saucier, add about 250 ml (8 fl oz) more stock.

Whole Tikka Cauliflower

SERVES 6

2 large cauliflowers
2 tablespoons flavourless oil
salt and pepper
handful of coriander, chopped, to serve

MARINADE

200 ml (7 fl oz) can coconut milk
3 tablespoons tomato purée
1 teaspoon chilli powder
1 teaspoon garam masala
1 teaspoon ground cumin
1 teaspoon ground coriander
finely grated zest and juice of 1 lemon
3 garlic cloves, finely grated

Mix together half the coconut milk with all the other ingredients for the marinade and rub it all over the cauliflowers. Set aside for at least 1 hour to marinate.

Season the cauliflowers well and drizzle the oil all over them. Roast on a baking tray in a preheated oven, 180°C (350°F), Gas Mark 4, for 40–45 minutes, with foil covering the top for the first 20 minutes to help the cauliflowers steam and cook through, before removing the foil so they can get caramelized and charred.

Serve with the remaining coconut milk, sprinkling with coriander, if you like.

TIP

You can leave out the ground spices and aromatics here and simply use a pot of vegan tikka curry paste mixed with the coconut milk and lemon zest to marinate the cauliflower if you prefer. Either way, to make it fancy, serve it with coriander.

Spicy Paneer with Tomatoes, Peas & Beans

SERVES 4

2 tablespoons vegetable oil
250 g (8 oz) paneer, diced
1 onion, finely chopped
2 garlic cloves, chopped
2 teaspoons peeled and finely grated fresh root ginger
1 teaspoon ground coriander
1 teaspoon paprika
1 teaspoon tomato purée
125 ml (4 fl oz) hot vegetable stock (see page 197 for homemade)
150 g (5 oz) French beans, topped and tailed
175 g (6 oz) frozen peas
150 g (5 oz) tomatoes, chopped
1 teaspoon garam masala
salt and pepper
chapattis, to serve

Heat half the oil in a large frying pan with a lid. Add the paneer, season well with salt and pepper and cook for 3–4 minutes until golden all over. Lift out with a slotted spoon on to a plate.

Add the remaining oil and the onion to the pan and cook for 5 minutes, until softened. Stir in the garlic and ginger and cook for a further 1 minute, then add the spices and cook for 30 seconds.

Stir in the tomato purée and stock, then add the beans and return the paneer to the pan. Season to taste with salt and pepper, cover and simmer for 5 minutes.

Add the peas and tomatoes and cook for a further 3 minutes, then stir in the garam masala. Divide among bowls and serve with chapattis.

Simple Fish Curry

££   >50

SERVES 4

40 g (1½ oz) fresh root ginger, peeled and grated
1 teaspoon ground turmeric
2 garlic cloves, crushed
2 teaspoons medium curry paste
150 ml (¼ pint) natural yogurt
625 g (1¼ lb) white fish fillets, skinned
2 tablespoons olive oil
1 large onion, sliced
1 cinnamon stick, halved
2 teaspoons dark muscovado sugar
2 bay leaves
400 g (13 oz) can chopped tomatoes
300 ml (½ pint) Fish Stock or Vegetable Stock
  (see page 197)
500 g (1 lb) waxy potatoes, cut into small chunks
25 g (1 oz) coriander, chopped
salt and pepper

Mix together the ginger, turmeric, garlic and curry paste in a bowl. Stir in the yogurt until combined. Cut the fish into large pieces and add to the bowl, stirring until coated in the spice mixture.

Heat the oil in a large saucepan and gently fry the onion, cinnamon, sugar and bay leaves until the onion is soft. Add the tomatoes, stock and potatoes and bring to the boil. Cook, uncovered, for about 20 minutes until the potatoes are tender and the sauce has thickened.

Tip in the fish and spicy yogurt and reduce the heat to its lowest setting. Cook gently for about 10 minutes or until the fish is cooked through. Check the seasoning and stir in the coriander to serve.

TIP
Once you've opened a jar of curry paste, don't leave it to rot at the back of the fridge. Use it up in one of the recipes on pages 63, 133, 148 and 174.

Tandoori Chicken

££ >20

SERVES 4

4 skinless chicken breast fillets
100 ml (3½ fl oz) natural yogurt
1 garlic clove, crushed
2 teaspoons peeled and finely grated fresh
   root ginger
2 tablespoons tandoori curry paste
1 onion, cut into wedges
2 tablespoons vegetable oil
2 tomatoes, quartered
15 g (½ oz) butter, cut into small pieces
salt and pepper

TO SERVE

lime wedges
ready-made or homemade raita (see tip)
warm naan bread

Line a baking sheet with foil and set a wire rack on top. Make 3 slashes across each chicken breast. Mix together the yogurt, garlic, ginger and tandoori paste and season well. Rub all over the chicken and leave to marinate for 5–10 minutes.

Toss the onion and chicken with the oil, then arrange on the rack. Place in a preheated oven, 230°C (450°F), Gas Mark 8, for 7 minutes.

Add the tomatoes, scatter over the butter and return to the oven for a further 5–10 minutes until the chicken is charred and just cooked through. Serve with lime wedges, raita and naan.

TIP

For homemade raita, mix 175 ml (6 fl oz) natural yogurt with 75 g (3 oz) deseeded and grated cucumber, 2 tablespoons chopped mint, a pinch of cumin, and salt and lemon juice to taste.

Chilli Con Veggie

SERVES 8–10

3 tablespoons extra virgin olive oil or regular olive oil
500 g (1 lb) chestnut mushrooms, finely chopped
1 large onion, finely chopped
1 celery stick, finely chopped
3 garlic cloves, finely chopped or crushed
1 red chilli, finely chopped, deseeded if you prefer less heat
2 teaspoons ground cumin
2 teaspoons ground coriander
1 teaspoon smoked paprika
2 tablespoons vegan bouillon powder
1 teaspoon caster sugar
2 x 400 g (13 oz) cans chopped tomatoes
2 x 400 g (13 oz) cans red kidney beans, drained and rinsed
salt and pepper

TO SERVE (OPTIONAL)

1–2 avocados, halved, peeled, pitted and finely sliced
coriander sprigs
lime wedges

In a large casserole dish or saucepan, heat the oil over a medium heat. Add the mushrooms and cook for 5-6 minutes until golden.

Add the onion and celery and cook for a further 10 minutes until translucent and soft. Add the garlic and chilli and cook for 1 minute, then add the ground spices and cook for 1 minute until fragrant.

Add the vegan bouillon powder, sugar and tomatoes. Bring to the boil, then reduce the heat to a simmer for 20-30 minutes until the sauce has begun to reduce. Add the beans and cook for a further 10 minutes, then taste and adjust the seasoning. Serve with avocado slices, coriander and lime wedges, if you like.

This will keep in the refrigerator for 4 days or, in portions, in the freezer for up to 6 months.

TIP

This gently spicy, incredibly hearty stew is great served over rice or used to load fries. You can really add whatever vegetables you have to hand; some finely chopped carrot, aubergine, courgette or red pepper would bulk it out further. You could also use any kind of bean here: cans of mixed beans are great, or swap out half the kidney beans for black beans, or make a white bean Chilli Con Veggie instead.

Chilli Con Carne

SERVES 4

4 tablespoons olive oil
2 red onions, finely chopped
6 garlic cloves, finely chopped
500 g (1 lb) lean minced beef
1 teaspoon ground cumin
2 small red peppers, cored, deseeded and diced
2 x 400 g (13 oz) cans chopped tomatoes
2 tablespoons tomato purée
1 tablespoon mild chilli powder
400 ml (14 fl oz) beef stock
2 x 400 g (13 oz) cans red kidney beans, rinsed
  and drained
salt and pepper
boiled rice, to serve

Heat the oil in a saucepan, add the onion and garlic and cook for 5 minutes until softened. Add the mince and cumin and cook for a further 5–6 minutes, or until browned all over.

Stir in the red pepper, tomatoes, tomato purée, chilli powder and stock and bring to the boil, then reduce the heat and simmer gently for 30 minutes.

Add the beans and cook for a further 5 minutes. Season to taste and serve with rice.

Chicken & Spinach Stew

SERVES 4

625 g (1¼ lb) boneless, skinless chicken thighs,
  thinly sliced
2 teaspoons ground cumin
1 teaspoon ground ginger
2 tablespoons olive oil
1 tablespoon tomato purée
2 x 400 g (13 oz) cans cherry tomatoes
50 g (2 oz) raisins
250 g (8 oz) ready-cooked Puy lentils
1 teaspoon finely grated lemon zest
150 g (5 oz) spinach leaves
salt and pepper
handful of chopped parsley, to garnish
steamed couscous boiled rice, to serve

Mix the chicken with the ground spices until well coated. Heat the oil in a large saucepan or flameproof casserole, then add the chicken and cook for 2–3 minutes until lightly browned.

Stir in the tomato purée, tomatoes, raisins, lentils and lemon zest. Season with salt and pepper and simmer gently, stirring occasionally, for about 12 minutes until thickened slightly and the chicken is cooked.

Add the spinach and stir until wilted. Ladle the stew into bowls, then scatter with the parsley and serve with steamed couscous or rice.

Veggie Goulash with Chive Dumplings

£   Veggie   >50

SERVES 4

4 tablespoons olive oil
8 baby onions
2 garlic cloves, crushed
1 carrot, chopped
1 large celery stick, sliced
500 g (1 lb) potatoes, cubed
1 teaspoon caraway seeds
1 teaspoon smoked paprika
400 g (13 oz) can chopped tomatoes
450 ml (¾ pint) vegetable stock (see page 197)
salt and pepper

CHIVE DUMPLINGS

75 g (3 oz) self-raising flour
½ teaspoon salt
50 g (2 oz) vegetarian suet
1 tablespoon chopped chives
4–5 tablespoons water

Heat the oil in a large saucepan, add the onions, garlic, carrot, celery, potatoes and caraway seeds and cook over a medium heat, stirring frequently, for 10 minutes. Add the paprika and cook, stirring, for 1 minute.

Stir in the tomatoes, stock and salt and pepper. Bring to the boil, then reduce the heat, cover and simmer gently for 20 minutes.

Make the dumplings. Sift the flour and salt into a bowl and stir in the suet, chives and pepper to taste. Working quickly and lightly, gradually mix in enough of the measured water to form a soft dough. Divide into 8 equal pieces and roll into balls.

Carefully arrange the dumplings in the stew, leaving gaps between them, cover and simmer for 15 minutes until doubled in size and light and fluffy.

Quick One-Pot Ratatouille

£ **Vegan** **>20**

SERVES 4

100 ml (3½ fl oz) olive oil
2 onions, chopped
1 medium aubergine, cut into bite-sized cubes
2 large courgettes, cut into bite-sized pieces
1 red pepper, cored, deseeded and cut into bite-sized pieces
1 yellow pepper, cored, deseeded and cut into bite-sized pieces
2 garlic cloves, crushed
400 g (13 oz) can chopped tomatoes
4 tablespoons chopped parsley or basil
salt and pepper

Heat the oil in a large saucepan until very hot, add the onions, aubergine, courgettes, peppers and garlic and cook, stirring constantly, for a few minutes until softened. Add the tomatoes, season to taste with salt and pepper and stir well.

Reduce the heat, cover the pan tightly and simmer for 15 minutes until all the vegetables are cooked.

Remove from the heat and stir in the chopped parsley or basil before serving.

Pork & Leek Stew

SERVES 4–5

1 kg (2 lb) boneless lean pork, diced
2 tablespoons vegetable oil
1 large onion, chopped
500 g (1 lb) leeks, trimmed, cleaned and chopped
3 bay leaves
1.5 litres (2½ pints) chicken or beef stock
75 g (3 oz) pearl barley
150 g (5 oz) self-raising flour
75 g (3 oz) beef or vegetable suet
about 125 ml (4 fl oz) water
150 g (5 oz) pitted prunes, halved
salt and pepper

Season the pork with plenty of salt and pepper. Heat 1 tablespoon of the oil in a large flameproof casserole and fry the pork in batches until browned on all sides, lifting out with a slotted spoon on to a plate.

Add the remaining oil to the casserole and gently fry the onion and leeks for 5 minutes. Return the pork to the casserole, add the bay leaves and stock and bring to a simmer. Stir in the pearl barley. Cover, reduce the heat to its lowest setting and cook for 1½ hours until the pork and barley are tender and the cooking juices have thickened.

Mix together the flour, suet and a little salt and pepper in a bowl. Add the measured water and mix with a round-bladed knife to a soft dough, adding a dash more water if the mixture feels dry and crumbly, but don't make it too sticky.

Stir the prunes into the stew and season to taste with salt and pepper. Using a dessertspoon, place spoonfuls of the dumpling mixture on the surface of the stew, spacing them slightly apart. Re-cover and cook gently for a further 15–20 minutes until the dumplings have risen and have a fluffy texture. Serve in shallow bowls.

Chorizo & Chickpea Stew

SERVES 4

1 teaspoon olive oil
2 red onions, chopped
2 red peppers, cored, deseeded and chopped
100 g (3½ oz) chorizo sausage, thinly sliced
500 g (1 lb) cooked new potatoes, sliced
500 g (1 lb) plum tomatoes, chopped, or 400 g
  (13 oz) can chopped tomatoes, drained
400 g (13 oz) can chickpeas, rinsed and drained
2 tablespoons chopped parsley, to garnish
garlic bread, to serve

Heat the oil in a large frying pan and fry the onions and red peppers over a medium heat for 3–4 minutes. Add the chorizo and cook, turning frequently, for 2 minutes.

Stir the potatoes, tomatoes and chickpeas into the pan and bring to the boil. Reduce the heat and cook gently for 10 minutes. Garnish with the chopped parsley and serve with garlic bread to mop up all the juices.

Broccoli Stir-Fry

£ | Vegan | <20

SERVES 2

2 tablespoons sesame oil or flavourless oil
1 red onion, finely sliced
1 garlic clove, finely chopped or crushed
20 g (¾ oz) fresh root ginger, peeled and grated
1 broccoli head, broken into florets, stalk finely sliced
1 red pepper, cored, deseeded and finely sliced
50 g (2 oz) cashew nuts
50 ml (2 fl oz) soy sauce
1 tablespoon maple syrup
finely grated zest and juice of 1 lime
lime wedges, to serve

Heat the oil in a wok, then add the onion, garlic and ginger and cook over a high heat for 2–3 minutes until golden.

Add the broccoli, red pepper and cashew nuts and stir-fry for 2–3 minutes more until beginning to gain colour and tenderize.

Add the soy sauce, maple syrup and lime zest and juice and cook for 1 minute until the sauce bubbles up and coats all the vegetables. Serve with lime wedges.

TIP

Don't throw your broccoli stalk away! It is great for bulking out this stir-fry, adds another texture and has a very intense broccoli flavour. If you don't want to use cashew nuts, simply leave them out.

Vegetable & Tofu Stir-Fry

SERVES 4

3 tablespoons sunflower oil
300 g (10 oz) firm tofu, cubed
1 onion, sliced
2 carrots, sliced
150 g (5 oz) broccoli, broken into small florets and
    stalks sliced
1 red pepper, cored, deseeded and sliced
1 large courgette, sliced
150 g (5 oz) sugar snap peas
2 tablespoons soy sauce
2 tablespoons sweet chilli sauce
125 ml (4 fl oz) water

TO GARNISH

2 red chillies, chopped
basil leaves

Heat 1 tablespoon of the oil in a wok until starting to smoke, add the tofu and stir-fry over a high heat for 2 minutes, or until golden. Lift out with a slotted spoon on to a plate.

Heat the remaining oil in the wok, add the onion and carrots and stir-fry for 1½ minutes. Add the broccoli and red pepper and stir-fry for 1 minute, then add the courgette and sugar snap peas and stir-fry for 1 minute.

Combine the soy and chilli sauces and the measured water in a mug, pour into the wok, then return the tofu to the wok and cook for 1 minute. Divide among bowls and garnish with the chopped red chillies and basil leaves.

Pesto Puff Tart

SERVES 4

375 g (12 oz) pack ready-rolled puff pastry
3 tablespoons shop-bought fresh green pesto
300 g (10 oz) yellow and red cherry tomatoes,
    halved
150 g (5 oz) mixed antipasti (artichokes, roasted
    peppers, mushrooms and aubergines), from a
    jar, drained
100 g (3½ oz) goats' cheese, crumbled
basil leaves, to garnish

Lay the puff pastry on a baking sheet. Score a 2.5 cm (1 inch) margin around the edge and prick the base with a fork.

Top with the pesto, tomatoes, mixed antipasti and goats' cheese. Bake in a preheated oven, 200°C (400°F), Gas Mark 6, for 15–20 minutes. Garnish with the basil leaves and serve.

TIP
Price comparison websites help you quickly locate the cheapest prices for your groceries. Forget about brand loyalty – follow the bargains to stretch your budget.

Chickpeas & Greens

SERVES 6–8

3 tablespoons olive oil
1 large red onion, finely sliced
2 garlic cloves, finely chopped or crushed
1 teaspoon sweet paprika
½ teaspoon ground cumin
½ teaspoon ground cinnamon
2 x 400 g (13 oz) cans chickpeas
400 g (13 oz) can chopped tomatoes
400 g (13 oz) leafy greens, such as kale, chard or
    spinach, coarse ribs removed
50 g (2 oz) raisins or sultanas
salt and pepper
chopped parsley, to serve (optional)

Heat the oil in a large, heavy-based saucepan. Add the onion and cook it, without browning, over a medium-low heat for 8–10 minutes until soft and translucent.

Add the garlic and cook for 2 minutes, then add the spices and cook for a further 1 minute.

Tip in the chickpeas and their liquid as well as the chopped tomatoes. Bring to the boil, then reduce the heat to a simmer for 20 minutes until reduced and thickened.

Add the greens (unless you plan to freeze the stew – see tip) and raisins and season well. Cook for 5–10 minutes more until the greens are wilted and cooked through. Taste and adjust the seasoning. Scatter with plenty of parsley, if you like, and serve.

TIP

If you plan to freeze it in small batches, do so before adding the greens; wilt these in only once the stew has defrosted and been reheated, to retain their nutritive value and bright colour.

Spiced Chickpeas & Kale

SERVES 4

3 tablespoons vegetable oil
3 red onions, cut into wedges
2 tablespoons mild curry paste
400 g (13 oz) can chopped tomatoes
400 g (13 oz) can chickpeas, rinsed and drained
300 ml (½ pint) vegetable stock (see page 197)
2 teaspoons soft light brown sugar
100 g (3½ oz) kale, tough talks removed
salt and pepper

Heat the oil in a large saucepan and fry the onions for 5 minutes, or until beginning to colour. Stir in the curry paste and then the tomatoes, chickpeas, stock and sugar. Bring to the boil, then reduce the heat, cover and simmer gently for 20 minutes.

Stir in the kale and cook gently for a further 10 minutes. Season to taste with salt and pepper and serve.

Charred Cauliflower Steaks with Herby Garlic Crumbs & Roasted Pepper Dip

£ — **Vegan** — **>20**

SERVES 6

2 large cauliflowers, each sliced into 3 fat 'steaks' with the root attached
3 tablespoons extra virgin olive oil or regular olive oil
1 quantity Roasted Red Pepper Dip (see page 212)
1 quantity Chilli, Lemon & Herb Crumbs, with parsley (see below)
salt and pepper

Lay the cauliflower steaks on a baking tray lined with baking paper. Coat well in the olive oil, being careful with the steaks as they can be quite delicate. Season well with salt and pepper and roast in a preheated oven to 220°C (425°F), Gas Mark 7, for 20–25 minutes, flipping halfway through and cooking until the steaks are charred and tender. Add the cauliflower leaves for the last 5–10 minutes.

Spread the red pepper dip on a large serving platter, top with the cauliflower steaks and sprinkle the flavoured crumbs over everything.

TIP
These steaks look beautifully burnished on top of their vibrant orange dip. Perfect in the summertime, if you can cook the cauliflower on a barbecue.

Chilli, Lemon & Herb Crumbs

£ — **Vegan** — **<20**

SERVES 6

50 ml (2 fl oz) olive oil
150 g (5 oz) breadcrumbs (or see tip)
1 tablespoon chilli flakes
finely grated zest of 1 lemon
1 tablespoon chopped herbs (try thyme, parsley or rosemary)

Heat the oil in a large frying pan and toss in the breadcrumbs. Fry for 3–4 minutes until golden and crisp.

Turn off the heat, then stir in the chilli flakes, lemon zest and herbs. Allow to cool, then store in an airtight container for up to 1 week.

TIP
This can be made from stale bread whizzed up in a food processor – a delicious way to jazz up pasta and salads.

DIY Baked Beans

>20

SERVES 6

1 tablespoon flavourless oil
1 shallot, finely chopped
1 large garlic clove, crushed
2 x 400 g (13 oz) cans cannellini beans, or other white beans, drained and rinsed
250 ml (8 fl oz) tomato passata
200 ml (7 fl oz) water or vegan stock
1 tablespoon caster sugar, or to taste
1–2 tablespoons apple cider vinegar, or to taste
salt and pepper

Heat the oil in a medium saucepan over a medium-low heat. Add the shallot and cook for 6–8 minutes until soft and translucent, then add the garlic and cook for 1 minute.

Add the beans, passata and measured water or stock and bring to the boil. Reduce the heat to a bare simmer, add the sugar and vinegar and cook for 10–15 minutes until the sauce has reduced slightly.

Taste and adjust the seasoning accordingly, adding more sugar or vinegar depending on your preference.

TIP
One of the quickest dishes you can make and it beats a canned version any day!

Sticky Sweet Aubergines

>20

SERVES 4

flavourless oil, for deep-frying
2 large aubergines, peeled and cut into small wedges
6 tablespoons miso paste
4 tablespoons soy sauce
2 tablespoons caster sugar
2 tablespoons rice wine vinegar or lime juice

TO SERVE

white rice
grated carrot
sesame seeds
small handful of coriander, roughly chopped

TIP
Make a big batch, scaling up depending on how many aubergines you have, then serve them over rice, stirred into noodles or as part of a salad bowl.

Heat enough oil for frying in a saucepan, about 5 cm (2 inch) deep, over a medium-high heat until the oil shimmers. Add the aubergines, in batches, and cook for 10–12 minutes until golden and softened.

Meanwhile, whisk together the miso, soy sauce, sugar and vinegar or lime juice, then pour on to a baking tray.

Use a slotted spoon to remove the aubergines from the hot oil and place straight on the baking tray. Toss the aubergines in the sauce, then bake in a preheated oven to 200°C (400°F), Gas Mark 6, for 10 minutes until the sauce has become sticky and caramelized.

Serve immediately with white rice and grated carrot, and sprinkled with sesame seeds and coriander, or store in an airtight container in the refrigerator for up to 3 days.

Classic Cheese Fondue

££ | Veggie | <20

SERVES 4

1 garlic clove, halved
200 ml (7 fl oz) dry white wine
2 teaspoons vinegar or lemon juice
1½ tablespoons cornflour
4 tablespoons kirsch, brandy, vodka or dry
   white wine
750 g (1½ lb) mixture of cheese (such as
   Emmental, Gruyère and mature Cheddar
   cheese, grated)
selection of dippers, such as cubes of crusty
   bread, raw vegetables (carrot and celery sticks,
   broccoli and cauliflower florets, halved mushrooms,
   cherry tomatoes), cooked sausages, pickled onions,
   cornichons and new potatoes, to serve

Rub the cut side of the garlic all over the inside of a saucepan, then discard. Pour in the wine and vinegar or lemon juice and bring to the boil. Meanwhile, stir the cornflour into the kirsch, brandy, vodka or wine until smooth.

Reduce the heat slightly so that the wine is simmering gently, then pour the kirsch into the wine in a slow, steady drizzle, stirring constantly for 1–2 minutes until thickened slightly.

Now stir in the cheese, a handful at a time, stirring constantly and waiting until the cheese has melted before adding more. Once all of the cheese has been combined and the fondue is smooth and thick, scrape into a warmed fondue dish and place on a lit fondue base following manufacturer's instructions.

Serve the fondue with a selection of dippers.

TIP

If you don't have a proper fondue dish, transfer the saucepan directly to the table, placing it on a heatproof mat or board. You may need to reheat the pan gently from time to time as the fondue cools.

Chicken Breasts with Mascarpone & Tomatoes

£££   >20

SERVES 4

4 tablespoons mascarpone cheese
4 teaspoons shop-bought fresh green pesto
4 skinless chicken breast fillets
100 g (3½ oz) dried breadcrumbs
3 tablespoons olive oil
150 g (5 oz) cherry tomatoes
25 g (1 oz) toasted pine nuts
salt and pepper
crusty bread, to serve (optional)

Mix together the mascarpone and pesto in a bowl. Cut a horizontal slit in the side of each chicken breast to form a pocket. Fill the pockets with the mascarpone mixture.

Spread out the breadcrumbs on a plate. Season the chicken breasts with salt and pepper, rub them with 1 tablespoon of the oil and then roll them in the breadcrumbs until well coated.

Place the chicken breasts in a roasting tin, drizzle over another tablespoon of the oil and bake in a preheated oven, 200°C (400°F), Gas Mark 6, for 10 minutes.

Add the tomatoes to the tin, season with salt and pepper and drizzle with the remaining oil. Return to the oven for a further 5 minutes, or until the chicken is cooked through. Scatter over the pine nuts and serve with crusty bread, if liked.

CHICKEN

Chicken Fajitas with No-Chilli Salsa

>20

SERVES 4

½ teaspoon ground coriander
½ teaspoon ground cumin
½ teaspoon paprika
1 garlic clove, crushed
3 tablespoons chopped coriander
375 g (12 oz) boneless, skinless chicken breasts
1 tablespoon olive oil
4 soft flour tortillas

SALSA

3 ripe tomatoes, finely chopped
3 tablespoons chopped coriander
⅛ cucumber, finely chopped
1 tablespoon olive oil

GUACAMOLE

1 large ripe avocado, peeled, pitted and chopped
finely grated zest and juice of ½ lime
sweet chilli sauce, to taste (optional)

To make the chicken fajitas, place all the ground spices, garlic and chopped coriander in a mixing bowl. Cut the chicken into bite-sized strips and toss in the oil, then add to the spices and toss to coat lightly in the spice mixture.

Make the salsa. Mix the tomatoes, coriander and cucumber in a bowl and drizzle over the oil. Transfer to a serving bowl.

Make the guacamole. Mash the avocado in a bowl with the lime zest and juice and sweet chilli sauce, if using, until soft and rough-textured.

Heat a griddle pan or heavy-based frying pan until hot and cook the chicken for 3–4 minutes, turning occasionally, until golden and cooked through. Top the tortillas with the hot chicken strips, guacamole and salsa, and fold into quarters to serve.

Pot Roast Chicken

>50

SERVES 4

1.5 kg (3 lb) oven-ready chicken
25 g (1 oz) butter
2 tablespoons olive oil
1 onion, sliced
3 celery sticks, sliced
4–6 garlic cloves, crushed
250 ml (8 fl oz) dry white wine
3 bay leaves
sprigs of thyme
150 g (5 oz) Puy lentils
2 tablespoons drained capers
4 tablespoons chopped parsley
100 ml (3½ fl oz) half-fat crème fraîche
salt and pepper

TIP

This dish makes a delightful change from a traditional roast chicken. If you have any leftover chicken, mix with mayo and shredded lettuce for an easy sandwich filling.

Season the chicken all over with salt and pepper. Melt the butter with the oil in a frying pan and fry the chicken on all sides. Transfer to a large, ovenproof casserole.

Fry the onion and celery in the pan juices for 6–8 minutes or until browned. Stir in the garlic, wine and herbs and pour over the chicken. Cover and bake in a preheated oven, 160°C (325°F), Gas Mark 3, for 1 hour.

Meanwhile, rinse the lentils and put them in a saucepan with plenty of water. Bring to the boil and boil for 10 minutes. Drain well.

Tip the lentils around the chicken and return to the oven for a further 45 minutes. Transfer the cooked chicken and lentil mixture to a warmed serving dish and cover. Remember to remove the bay leaves and thyme sprigs before serving.

Mix the capers, parsley and crème fraîche together in a small pan and heat through gently, stirring. Serve with the carved chicken and the lentil mixture.

Chicken & Vegetable Stir-Fry

££   <20

SERVES 4

2 tablespoons coconut oil
3 cm (1¼ inches) piece of fresh root ginger, peeled and finely diced
2 garlic cloves, crushed
1 onion, chopped
450 g (14½ oz) chicken breast fillets, cut into strips
125 g (4 oz) mushrooms, quartered
300 g (10 oz) broccoli florets
125 g (4 oz) curly kale, chopped
1–2 tablespoons soy sauce
2 tablespoons sesame seeds

Heat the oil in a wok or large frying pan until hot, add the ginger, garlic and onion and stir-fry for 30 seconds. Add the chicken and stir-fry for a further 2–3 minutes.

Add the vegetables, then sprinkle over the soy sauce. Stir-fry for 1–2 minutes, then cover and steam for a further 4–5 minutes until the vegetables are tender and the chicken is cooked through.

Serve sprinkled with the sesame seeds.

TIP

This quick and easy stir-fry includes 'queen of greens' kale, plus broccoli which is high in choline to help boost the growth of brain cells.

Chicken, Olive & Cumin Couscous

££

<20

SERVES 4

4 tablespoons olive oil
zest and flesh of ½ lemon, finely chopped
1 tablespoon honey
½ teaspoon ground cumin
1 garlic clove, crushed
300 g (10 oz) couscous
300 ml (½ pint) hot chicken stock (see page 197)
400 g (13 oz) can chickpeas, rinsed and drained
50 g (2 oz) green olives, pitted
2 ready-cooked chicken breasts, sliced
handful each of chopped coriander and mint,
    finely chopped
salt and pepper

Heat the oil in a saucepan, add the lemon and cook over a gentle heat for about 2 minutes until the lemon is soft. Stir in the honey, cumin and garlic and heat through. Stir in the couscous, stock, chickpeas, olives and chicken.

Remove from the heat and leave to stand for 5 minutes, or until the couscous is tender. Fluff up the couscous with a fork and stir in the coriander and mint. Season to taste with salt and pepper and serve immediately.

Lemon Chilli Chicken

££

>50

SERVES 4

1 chicken, about 1.75 kg (3½ lb), jointed
8 garlic cloves
4 juicy lemons, quartered and squeezed,
    skins reserved
1 small red chilli, deseeded and chopped
2 tablespoons orange blossom honey
4 tablespoons chopped parsley, plus sprigs to
    garnish
salt and pepper

Arrange the chicken pieces in a shallow, flameproof casserole. Crush 2 of the garlic cloves, then put them in a mug with the lemon juice, chilli and honey and stir well. Pour the mixture over the chicken. Tuck the lemon skins around the meat, cover with clingfilm and leave to marinate in the fridge for at least 2 hours or overnight, turning once or twice.

Turn the chicken pieces skin-side up, scatter over the remaining whole garlic cloves and place the lemon skins, cut-side down, on top. Cook the chicken in a preheated oven, 200°C (400°F), Gas Mark 6, for 45 minutes, or until golden brown, cooked through and tender. Stir in the parsley, season to taste with salt and pepper and serve garnished with sprigs of parsley.

Caribbean Chicken with Rice & Peas

££   >20

SERVES 2

2 teaspoons jerk seasoning

1 teaspoon peeled and grated fresh root ginger

juice of 1 lime

2 boneless, skinless chicken breasts, about 150 g (5 oz) each

3 tablespoons vegetable oil

1 small onion, chopped

1 garlic clove, crushed

150 g (5 oz) long-grain rice

175 ml (6 fl oz) chicken stock (see page 197)

175 ml (6 fl oz) coconut milk

200 g (7 oz) can red kidney beans, rinsed and drained

50 g (2 oz) frozen or canned sweetcorn

few thyme sprigs, plus extra to garnish

lime wedges, to serve

Mix together the jerk seasoning, ginger and lime juice in a non-metallic bowl. Cut a few slashes across each chicken breast and coat in the mixture. Heat 2 tablespoons of the oil in a frying pan, add the chicken and cook over a medium heat for 15–20 minutes, turning occasionally, until cooked through.

Meanwhile, heat the remaining oil in a saucepan, add the onion and garlic and cook for 2 minutes until slightly softened. Add the rice, stock and coconut milk and bring to the boil, then reduce the heat, cover and simmer for 15–20 minutes until the liquid has been absorbed and the rice is tender, adding the kidney beans, sweetcorn and thyme sprigs for the final 5 minutes.

Slice the chicken and serve with the rice mixture and lime wedges, garnished with a few sprigs of thyme.

Chicken Drumstick Jambalaya

££   >20

SERVES 4

1 tablespoon sunflower oil

8 skinless chicken drumsticks

1 onion, chopped

2 garlic cloves, crushed

2 celery sticks, sliced

1 red chilli, deseeded and chopped

1 green pepper, cored, deseeded and chopped

75 g (3 oz) chorizo sausage, sliced

250 g (8 oz) long-grain rice

500 ml (17 fl oz) chicken stock (see page 197)

1 bay leaf

3 tomatoes, cut into wedges

dash of Tabasco sauce

salt and pepper

Heat the oil in a large saucepan. Cut a few slashes across the thickest part of the drumsticks, add them to the pan and fry over a high heat for 5 minutes, turning occasionally. Add the onion, garlic, celery, chilli and green pepper and cook for a further 2–3 minutes until softened.

Add the chorizo, fry briefly, then add the rice, stirring to coat the grains in the pan juices. Pour in the stock, add the bay leaf and bring to the boil. Cover, reduce the heat and simmer for 20 minutes, stirring occasionally, until the stock has been absorbed and the rice is tender.

Stir in the tomatoes and Tabasco sauce and season to taste with salt and pepper. Heat through for 3 minutes before serving.

Meatballs with Tomato Sauce

SERVES 4

500 g (1 lb) lean minced beef
3 garlic cloves, crushed
2 small onions, finely chopped
25 g (1 oz) breadcrumbs
40 g (1½ oz) Parmesan cheese, grated
6 tablespoons olive oil
100 ml (3½ fl oz) red wine
2 x 400 g (13 oz) cans chopped tomatoes
1 teaspoon caster sugar
3 tablespoons sun-dried tomato paste
75 g (3 oz) pitted Italian black olives, roughly
   chopped
4 tablespoons roughly chopped oregano
125 g (4 oz) mozzarella cheese, thinly sliced
salt and pepper
warm crusty bread, to serve

Put the beef in a bowl with half the crushed garlic and half the onion, the breadcrumbs and 25 g (1 oz) of the Parmesan. Season and use your hands to thoroughly blend the ingredients together. Shape into small balls, about 2.5 cm (1 inch) in diameter.

Heat half the oil in a large frying pan and fry the meatballs, shaking the pan frequently, for about 10 minutes until browned. Lift out with a slotted spoon onto a plate.

Add the remaining oil and onion to the pan and fry until softened. Add the wine and let the mixture bubble until the wine has almost evaporated. Stir in the remaining garlic, the tomatoes, sugar, tomato paste and a little seasoning. Bring to the boil and let the mixture bubble until slightly thickened.

Stir in the olives, all but 1 tablespoon of the oregano and the meatballs. Cook gently for a further 5 minutes.

Arrange the mozzarella slices over the top and scatter with the remaining oregano and Parmesan. Season with pepper and cook under a preheated grill until the cheese starts to melt. Serve in bowls with warm crusty bread.

Beef & Potato Hash

SERVES 4

2 tablespoons vegetable oil
750 g (1½ lb) minced beef
1 fennel bulb, trimmed and chopped
2 celery sticks, chopped
2 teaspoons cornflour
450 ml (¾ pint) beef stock
3 tablespoons tomato purée
700 g (1 lb 7 oz) waxy potatoes, cut into 1.5 cm
  (¾ inch) chunks
4 star anise, broken into pieces and crushed using
  a pestle and mortar (or a rolling pin or empty
  wine bottle)
3 tablespoons soy sauce
1 tablespoon light muscovado sugar
15 g (½ oz) coriander, roughly chopped
salt and pepper

Heat 1 tablespoon of the oil in a large heavy-based frying pan with a lid and fry the beef for 10 minutes, breaking up the mince with a wooden spoon and stirring until browned and all the moisture has evaporated. Push the meat to one side of the pan, add the remaining oil, fennel and celery and fry for 5 minutes, or until softened.

Blend the cornflour with a little of the stock in a mug, pour into the pan and stir to thicken. Add the remaining stock, tomato purée, potatoes and star anise and bring to a simmer, stirring. Reduce the heat, cover and cook gently for about 30 minutes until the potatoes are tender, stirring occasionally and adding a dash more water if the pan becomes dry.

Stir in the soy sauce and sugar and cook for a further 5 minutes, uncovered if necessary to thicken the juices. Season to taste with salt and pepper and stir in the coriander just before serving.

Shepherd's Pie

££ >50

SERVES 4–5

1 tablespoon olive oil
1 onion, finely chopped
1 carrot, diced
1 celery stick, diced
1 tablespoon chopped thyme
500 g (1 lb) minced lamb
400 g (13 oz) can chopped tomatoes
4 tablespoons tomato purée
750 g (1½ lb) floury potatoes, such as
   Desiree, peeled and cubed
50 g (2 oz) butter
3 tablespoons milk
75 g (3 oz) Cheddar cheese, grated
salt and pepper

Heat the oil in a saucepan, add the onion, carrot, celery and thyme and cook gently for 10 minutes until soft and golden.

Add the minced lamb and cook over a high heat, breaking up with a wooden spoon, for 5 minutes until browned. Add the tomatoes, tomato purée and salt and pepper to taste. Bring to the boil, then reduce the heat, cover and simmer for 30 minutes.

Remove the lid and cook for a further 15 minutes until thickened.

Meanwhile, put the potatoes in a large saucepan of lightly salted water and bring to the boil. Reduce the heat and simmer for 15–20 minutes until really tender. Drain well and return to the pan. Mash in the butter, milk and half the cheese and season to taste with salt and pepper.

Spoon the minced lamb mixture into an ovenproof dish and carefully spoon the mash over the top, spreading over the surface of the filling. Fork the top of the mash and scatter over the remaining cheese. Bake in a preheated oven, 190°C (375°F), Gas Mark 5, for 20–25 minutes until bubbling and golden.

Greek Lamb & Tzatziki Toasts

>50

SERVES 4

750 g (1½ lb) lamb chump chops
2 teaspoons dried oregano
3 garlic cloves, crushed
4 tablespoons olive oil
1 medium aubergine, about 300 g (10 oz), diced
2 red onions, sliced
200 ml (7 fl oz) white or red wine
400 g (13 oz) can chopped tomatoes
2 tablespoons honey
8 kalamata olives
8 thin slices French stick
200 g (7 oz) ready-made tzatziki
salt and pepper

Cut the lamb into large pieces, discarding any excess fat. Mix the oregano with the garlic and a little seasoning and rub into the lamb.

Heat half the oil in a large saucepan or frying pan and fry the lamb in batches until browned. Lift out with a slotted spoon onto a plate.

Add the aubergine to the pan with the onions and remaining oil and cook very gently, stirring frequently, for about 10 minutes until softened and lightly browned. Return the meat to the pan with the wine, tomatoes, honey, olives and seasoning. Cover with a lid and cook on the lowest setting for about 1¼ hours or until the lamb is very tender.

Lightly toast the bread and spoon the tzatziki on top.

Check the stew for seasoning and turn into bowls. Serve with the toasts on the side.

Garlicky Pork with Warm Butter Bean Salad

<20

SERVES 4

4 tablespoons olive oil
2 garlic cloves, crushed
4 lean pork chops or steaks, about 150 g (5 oz) each
salt and pepper

SALAD

2 tablespoons olive oil
2 x 400 g (13 oz) cans butter beans, rinsed and drained
12 cherry tomatoes, halved
150 ml (¼ pint) chicken stock (see page 197)
juice of 2 lemons
2 handfuls of parsley, chopped

Mix together the oil and garlic in a bowl, then season with salt and pepper. Place the pork on a foil-lined grill rack and spoon over the garlicky oil. Cook under a preheated medium grill for about 10 minutes, turning occasionally, until golden and cooked through.

Meanwhile, make the salad. Heat the oil in a large frying pan, add the butter beans and tomatoes and heat through for a few minutes. Add the stock, lemon juice and parsley and season with salt and pepper. Serve with the grilled chops or steaks.

Thai Red Pork & Bean Curry

££ <20

SERVES 4

2 tablespoons groundnut oil
1½ tablespoons Thai red curry paste
375 g (12 oz) lean pork, sliced into thin strips
100 g (3½ oz) green beans, trimmed and cut in half
2 tablespoons Thai fish sauce
1 teaspoon caster sugar
Chinese chives or regular chives, to garnish

Heat the oil in a wok or large frying pan over a medium heat until the oil starts to shimmer, add the curry paste and cook, stirring, until it releases its aroma.

Add the pork and beans and stir-fry for 2–3 minutes or until the meat is cooked through and the beans are just tender.

Stir in the fish sauce and sugar and serve, garnished with Chinese chives or regular chives.

TIP

Stir-fries are a brilliant way of making a little meat go a long way. Serve with steamed rice for a more filling meal, if you like.

Hoisin Pork Stir-Fry

££ <20

SERVES 4

1 tablespoon hoisin sauce
1 tablespoon light soy sauce
1 tablespoon white wine vinegar
1 tablespoon vegetable oil
2 garlic cloves, sliced
1 teaspoon peeled and grated fresh root ginger
1 small red chilli, deseeded and sliced
250 g (8 oz) pork fillet, thinly sliced
175 g (6 oz) sugar snap peas
175 g (6 oz) broccoli florets
2 tablespoons water
steamed rice, to serve

Combine the hoisin and soy sauces and vinegar in a mug and set aside.

Heat the oil in a wok until starting to smoke, add the garlic, ginger and chilli and stir-fry over a high heat for 10 seconds. Add the pork fillet and stir-fry for 2–3 minutes, or until golden. Lift out with a slotted spoon on to a plate.

Add the sugar snap peas and broccoli florets to the wok and stir-fry for 1 minute. Add the measured water and cook for a further 1 minute.

Return the pork to the wok, add the hoisin mixture and cook for 1 minute, or until the vegetables are cooked. Serve with steamed rice.

Spicy Sausage Bake

££

>50

SERVES 2

450 g (14½ oz) Italian sausages
2 tablespoons olive oil
1 large red onion, sliced
2 x 400 g (13 oz) cans chopped tomatoes
2 tablespoons chopped oregano
400 g (13 oz) can red kidney beans, rinsed
   and drained
200 g (7 oz) dried fusilli pasta
175 g (6 oz) fontina cheese, grated
salt

Slice each sausage into quarters. Heat the oil in a large, heavy-based frying pan and gently fry the sausages and onion for about 10 minutes until golden, gently shaking the pan frequently.

Add the tomatoes, oregano and red kidney beans. Reduce the heat to its lowest setting, cover and cook gently for 10 minutes.

Meanwhile, cook the pasta in a large saucepan of lightly salted boiling water for about 10 minutes or until just tender. Drain and tip into the frying pan. Add half of the cheese and toss the ingredients together until mixed. Tip the mixture into a 1.5 litre (2½ pint) shallow, ovenproof dish and scatter with the remaining cheese. Bake in a preheated oven, 200°C (400°F), Gas Mark 6, for 20–25 minutes or until the cheese is melting and golden.

Toad in the Hole

>20

SERVES 4

125 g (4 oz) plain flour
1 egg
300 ml (½ pint) milk or equal mixture of milk and
   water
500 g (1 lb) pork sausages
8 rindless bacon rashers
2 tablespoons vegetable oil
salt and pepper
baked beans or Irish champ (see tip), to serve
   (optional)

Put the flour and a dash of salt and pepper in a bowl, then crack in the egg. Slowly whisk in the milk or milk-and-water mixture until the batter is smooth and frothy.

Separate the sausages from each other. Stretch each rasher of bacon by laying it on a chopping board and running the flat edge of a knife along the rasher until it is half as long again. Wrap a rasher of bacon around each sausage.

Pour the oil into a roasting tin and add the bacon-wrapped sausages, keeping them spaced apart. Roast in a preheated oven, 220°C (425°F), Gas Mark 7, for 5 minutes until sizzling. Whisk the batter again.

TIP

Serve this with Irish champ. Cook 1.5 kg (3 lb) potatoes in lightly salted boiling water for 20 minutes, drain, return to the pan and mash. Beat in 150 ml (¼ pint) milk, 3 chopped spring onions, 50 g (2 oz) butter and season.

Take the roasting tin out of the oven and quickly pour in the batter, making sure that the sausages are still spaced apart. Return the tin to the oven and cook for about 20 minutes until the batter is risen and golden and the sausages are cooked through. Serve with baked beans or Irish champ (see tip), if liked.

Sausage & Onion Traybake

SERVES 4

3 red onions, cut into wedges
3 red apples, cored and cut into 6 wedges
200 g (7 oz) baby carrots, scrubbed
3 potatoes, peeled and cut into small cubes
4 tablespoons olive oil
12 pork sausages
2 tablespoons chopped sage
1 tablespoon rosemary
3 tablespoons honey
salt and pepper

Scatter the onions, apples, carrots and potatoes in a large roasting tin. Drizzle over the oil and toss well to lightly coat all the vegetables in the oil. Season generously with salt and pepper. Arrange the sausages in and around the vegetables, sprinkle over the herbs and toss again.

Bake in a preheated oven, 200°C (400°F), Gas Mark 6, for 20–22 minutes until golden and cooked through. Remove from the oven and drizzle over the honey. Toss all the vegetables and sausages in the honey and serve.

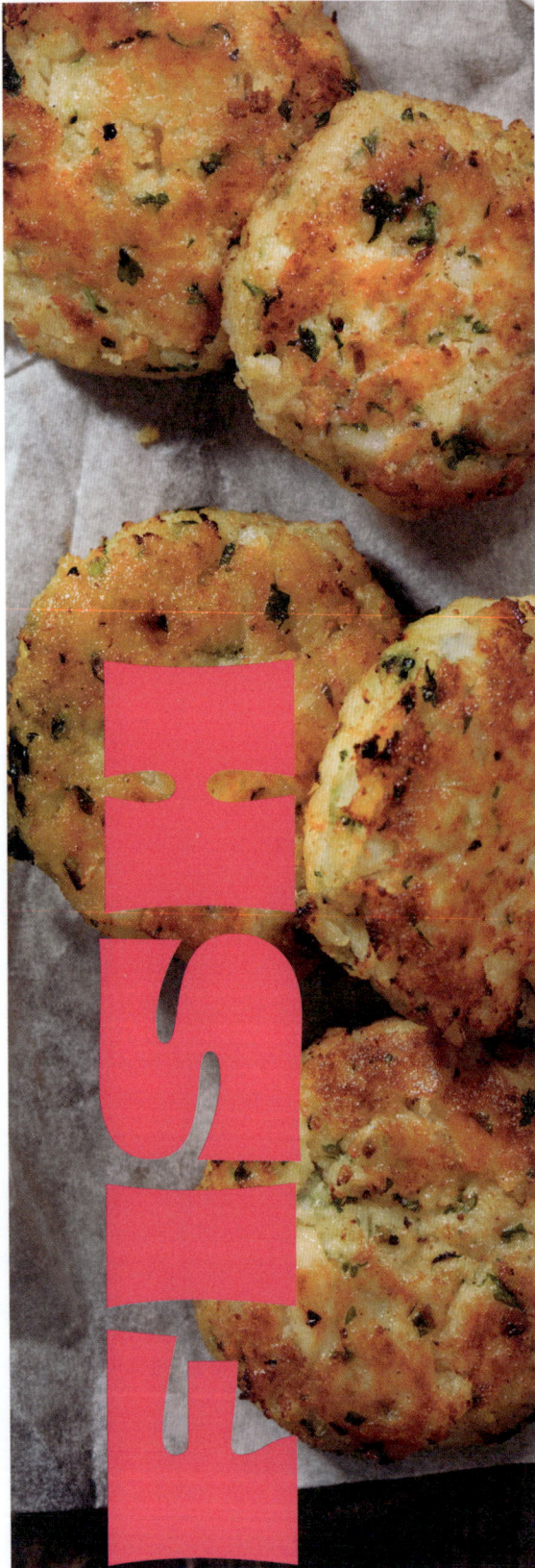

Thai-Style Crab Cakes with Salsa

£££ >20

SERVES 4

625 g (1¼ lb) fresh white crabmeat
400 g (13 oz) floury potatoes, cooked and mashed
2.5 cm (1 inch) piece of fresh root ginger, peeled and finely grated
grated zest of 1 lime
1 red chilli, deseeded and finely chopped
1 tablespoon mayonnaise
5 tablespoons vegetable oil, for shallow-frying
salt and pepper

BLACK-EYED BEAN SALSA

400 g (13 oz) can black-eyed beans, drained
1 red pepper, cored, deseeded and finely diced
300 g (10 oz) can sweetcorn, drained
3 tablespoons lime juice
2 tablespoons olive oil
2 tablespoons chopped coriander

Mix together the crab, potatoes, ginger, lime zest, chilli and mayonnaise. Season the mixture well with salt and pepper. Divide the mixture into 12 portions and shape into cakes with your hands.

Heat the vegetable oil in a frying pan and fry the crab cakes for 3–4 minutes on each side until they are golden brown.

Make the salsa by mixing together the beans, red pepper and sweetcorn. Squeeze over the lime juice and stir in the olive oil. Season with salt and pepper. Finally, mix in the chopped coriander.

FISH

Quick Tuna Fishcakes

£

>20

SERVES 4

250 g (8 oz) baking potatoes, peeled and diced
2 x 200 g (7 oz) cans tuna in olive oil, drained
50 g (2 oz) Cheddar cheese, grated
4 spring onions, finely chopped
1 small garlic clove, crushed
2 teaspoons dried thyme
1 small egg, beaten
½ teaspoon cayenne pepper, or to taste
4 tablespoons plain flour
vegetable oil, for frying
salt and pepper

TO SERVE

mixed green salad
mayonnaise

Cook the potatoes in a saucepan of lightly salted boiling water for 10 minutes or until tender. Drain well, mash and cool slightly.

Flake the tuna. Beat the tuna, cheese, spring onions, garlic, thyme and egg into the mashed potatoes. Season to taste with cayenne, salt and pepper.

Divide the mixture into 4 even portions and shape each one into a thick patty. Season the flour with salt and pepper, then dust the patties all over with the flour.

Heat a shallow layer of vegetable oil in a frying pan until hot, then fry the fishcakes for 5 minutes on each side or until crisp and golden. Serve hot with a mixed green salad and mayonnaise.

Mackerel & Sesame Noodles

££

<20

SERVES 2

2 large mackerel fillets, about 125 g (4 oz) each, cut into pieces
2 tablespoons teriyaki sauce
2 teaspoons sesame oil
1 tablespoon sesame seeds
½ bunch of spring onions, chopped
1 garlic clove, very thinly sliced
100 g (3½ oz) French beans, topped and tailed and diagonally sliced
400 ml (14 fl oz) Fish Stock (see page 197)
150 g (5 oz) pack medium straight-to-wok rice noodles
1 teaspoon caster sugar
1 teaspoon lime juice

Put the mackerel in a bowl with the teriyaki sauce and toss to coat the fish with the sauce.

Warm the oil in a saucepan, then add the sesame seeds, spring onions, garlic and beans and heat through gently for 2 minutes.

Pour in the stock and bring to a gentle simmer. Cover and cook for 5 minutes.

Stir the mackerel, noodles, sugar and lime juice into the pan and cook gently for 2 minutes, or until the mackerel is cooked and the broth is hot. Serve immediately.

Fish Pie

SERVES 4

750 g (1½ lb) floury potatoes, cut into chunks
2 eggs (optional)
400 ml (14 fl oz) full-fat milk
50 g (2 oz) plain flour
100 g (3½ oz) butter
2 tablespoons chopped parsley
25 g (1 oz) watercress, roughly chopped (optional)
200 g (7 oz) raw peeled king prawns
390 g (12¾ oz) shop-bought fish pie mixture
  (available from the chilled section of
  supermarkets), or use bite-sized chunks of
  salmon, white fish fillet and smoked haddock
3 tablespoons crème fraîche
75 g (3 oz) Cheddar cheese, grated
salt and pepper

Cook the potatoes in a pan of lightly salted boiling water for around 10–12 minutes, until tender.

Hard-boil the eggs, if using, in a pan of simmering water for about 8 minutes. Drain and hold under cold running water. Once cool enough to handle, remove the shells and cut the eggs into wedges.

Place the milk, flour and half the butter in a saucepan and bring slowly to the boil, stirring constantly with a balloon whisk, until thick and smooth. Simmer for 1–2 minutes, then season lightly and take off the heat.

Stir the parsley, watercress, if using, prawns, fish and egg into the sauce, then transfer to an ovenproof dish.

Drain the potatoes and mash them with the crème fraîche and the remaining butter. Season to taste, then spoon over the fish mixture and scatter with the grated cheese. Place the pie in a preheated oven, 220°C (425°F), Gas Mark 7, for 12–15 minutes, until golden and bubbling and the fish is cooked.

TIP
Whether you're lucky enough to have a dishwasher in your digs or you have to get down and dirty with the dishes, always rinse pots, pans and plates as soon as they've been used. That way, if the dishwashing fairies turn up late for their shift, the food won't have dried like a layer of cement and washing up will be easier.

Sugar & Spice Salmon

SERVES 4

3 tablespoons groundnut oil, plus extra for oiling
4 salmon fillets, about 200 g (7 oz) each
3 tablespoons light muscovado sugar
2 garlic cloves, crushed
1 teaspoon cumin seeds, crushed
1 teaspoon smoked or sweet paprika
1 tablespoon white wine vinegar
½ teaspoon cumin seeds, crushed
2 courgettes, cut into thin ribbons
salt and pepper
lemon or lime wedges, to serve

Put the salmon fillets in a lightly oiled roasting tin. Mix the sugar, garlic, cumin seeds, paprika, vinegar and a little salt in a bowl, then spread the mixture all over the fish so that it is thinly coated. Drizzle with 1 tablespoon of oil.

Bake in a preheated oven, 220°C (425°F), Gas Mark 7, for 10 minutes or until the fish is cooked through.

Heat the remaining oil in a large frying pan, add the cumin seeds and fry for 10 seconds. Add the courgette ribbons, season with salt and pepper and stir-fry for 2–3 minutes until just softened.

Serve the salmon garnished with lemon or lime wedges.

Rösti with Smoked Salmon & Rocket Salad

SERVES 4

750 g (1½ lb) waxy potatoes, coarsely grated
1 small onion, coarsely grated
50 g (2 oz) butter
3 tablespoons olive oil
2 tablespoons lemon juice
100 g (3½ oz) rocket
salt and pepper

TO SERVE

250 g (8 oz) smoked salmon
lemon wedges

Place the potatoes and onion in a clean tea towel and squeeze to remove excess moisture. Season well with salt and pepper.

Heat the butter and 1 tablespoon of the oil in a nonstick frying pan. Tip in the potato mixture and spread out to make an even layer, then cook for about 10 minutes, or until the underside is golden. Invert the rösti on to a plate, then carefully slide it back into the pan to cook the other side. Cook for a further 5–8 minutes until cooked through and golden all over.

Meanwhile, make the rocket salad. Mix the lemon juice with the remaining oil in a bowl and toss with the rocket.

Cut the rösti into wedges and serve with the rocket salad, slices of smoked salmon and lemon wedges.

££

Salmon with
Green Vegetables

>20

SERVES 4

1 tablespoon olive oil
1 leek, trimmed, cleaned and thinly sliced
275 ml (9 fl oz) Fish Stock (see page 197)
200 ml (7 fl oz) crème fraîche
125 g (4 oz) frozen peas
125 g (4 oz) frozen soya or broad beans
4 chunky skinless salmon fillets, about 150 g
  (5 oz) each
2 tablespoons snipped chives
pepper
Mashed Potato, to serve (see page 84)

Heat the oil in a large heavy-based frying pan with a lid and cook the leek over a medium heat, stirring frequently, for 3 minutes, or until softened. Pour in the stock, bring to the boil and continue boiling for 2 minutes, or until reduced a little.

Add the crème fraîche and stir well to mix. Add the peas, soya or broad beans and salmon and return to the boil. Reduce the heat, cover and simmer for 10 minutes, or until the fish is opaque and cooked through and the peas and beans are piping hot.

Sprinkle over the chives, season with pepper and serve spooned over mashed potato.

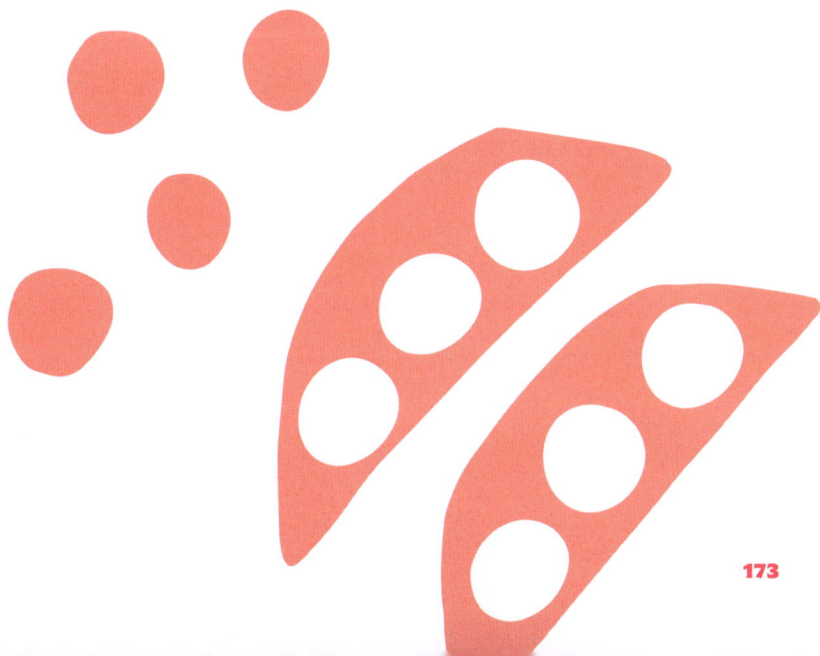

Spicy Prawn & Pea Pilau

>20

SERVES 4

1 tablespoon sunflower oil
1 tablespoon butter
1 large onion, finely chopped
2 garlic cloves, finely chopped
1 tablespoon medium or hot curry paste
250 g (8 oz) basmati rice
600 ml (1 pint) hot fish or vegetable stock (see page 197)
300 g (10 oz) frozen peas
finely grated zest and juice of 1 large lime
20 g (3/4 oz) fresh coriander, finely chopped
400 g (13 oz) ready-cooked peeled prawns
salt and pepper

Heat the oil and butter in a heavy-based saucepan, add the onion and cook over a medium heat for 2–3 minutes until softened. Stir in the garlic and curry paste and cook for a further 1–2 minutes until fragrant, then add the rice and stir to coat well.

Stir in the stock, peas and lime zest, then season well with salt and pepper and bring to the boil. Cover tightly, then reduce the heat to low and cook for 12–15 minutes until the liquid is absorbed and the rice is tender.

Remove from the heat, then stir in the lime juice, coriander and prawns. Cover and leave to stand for a few minutes to allow the prawns to heat through before serving.

Oven-Baked Fish & Chips with Tomato Salsa

>20

SERVES 4

750 g (1½ lb) potatoes, cut into thin wedges
4 tablespoons olive oil
4 skinless cod or haddock fillets
finely grated zest of 1 lemon
1 teaspoon balsamic vinegar
4 tomatoes, chopped
1 teaspoon drained capers
1 spring onion, chopped
salt and pepper
handful of chopped parsley, to garnish

Place the potatoes in a roasting tin. Drizzle over half the oil, season well with salt and pepper and toss to make sure the potatoes are coated in oil. Bake in a preheated oven, 220°C (425°F), Gas Mark 7, for 10 minutes.

Turn over the potatoes, place the fish on top, season again and scatter over the lemon zest. Return to the oven for a further 15–20 minutes until the potatoes are just cooked through.

Meanwhile, make the tomato salsa. Mix together the remaining oil and the vinegar in a bowl and season to taste with salt and pepper. Stir in the tomatoes, capers and spring onion.

Transfer the fish to plates, garnish with the chopped parsley and serve with the chips and salsa on the side.

desserts

Roasted Honey Peaches

>20

SERVES 4

2 tablespoons orange blossom honey
1 vanilla pod, split in half lengthways
2–3 teaspoons sesame seeds
4 peaches, halved and pitted
vanilla ice cream or crème fraîche, to serve
(optional)

Spoon the honey into a small saucepan. Scrape the seeds from the vanilla pod and add the seeds and pod to the pan. Heat gently, stirring occasionally for 1–2 minutes. Stir in the sesame seeds.

Place the peaches cut-side down in a roasting tin and pour over the honey mixture. Bake in a preheated oven, 180°C (350°F), Gas Mark 4, for 20–25 minutes until the peaches are soft. Baste a couple of times with the juices during cooking.

Serve the baked peaches warm with vanilla ice cream or crème fraîche, if liked.

Hot Caribbean Fruit Salad

<20

SERVES 4–5

50 g (2 oz) unsalted butter
50 g (2 oz) light muscovado sugar
1 large papaya, halved, deseeded, peeled and sliced
1 large mango, peeled, pitted and sliced
½ pineapple, skinned, cored and cut into chunks
400 ml (14 fl oz) can coconut milk
grated zest and juice of 1 lime

Melt the butter in a large frying pan, add the sugar and heat gently until just dissolved. Add all the fruit and cook for 2 minutes, then pour in the coconut milk and lime juice and add half the lime zest. Heat gently for 4–5 minutes, then serve warm in shallow bowls, sprinkled with the remaining lime zest.

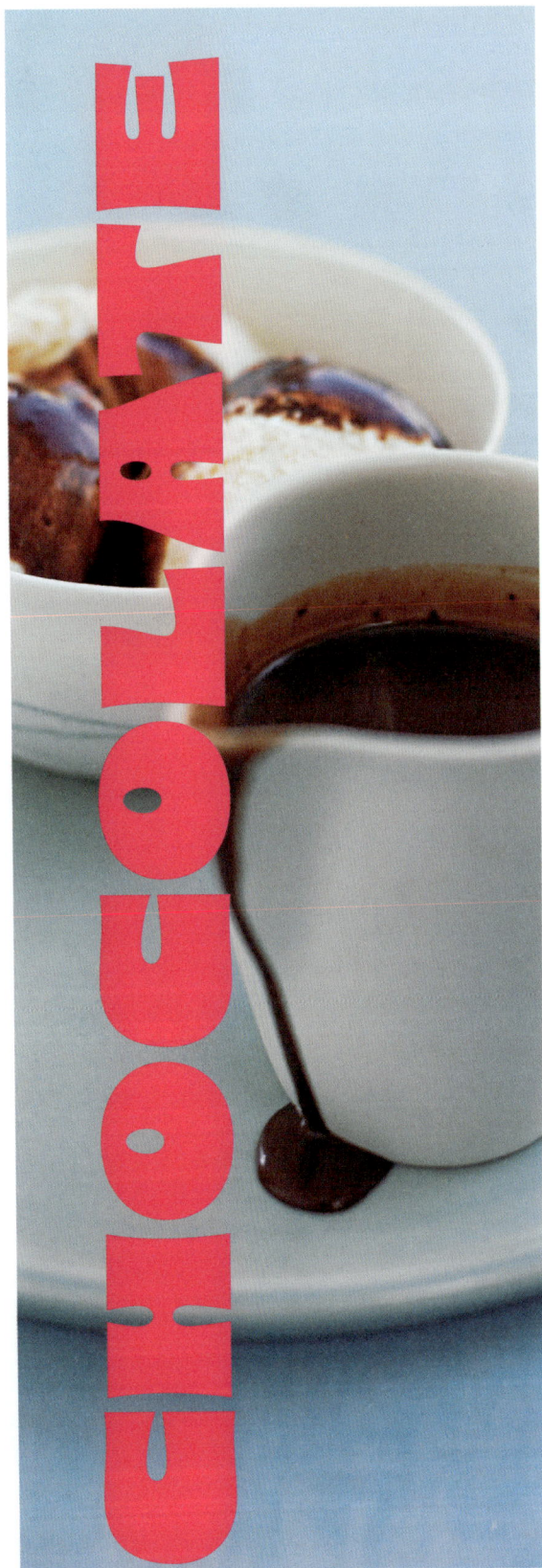

Easy Peasy Chocolate Sauce

£ | Veggie | <20

SERVES 4

175 g (6 oz) evaporated milk
100 g (3½ oz) plain dark chocolate, broken
   into pieces

Tip the evaporated milk into a pan, add the chocolate and heat gently for 2–3 minutes, stirring until the chocolate is melted.

Serve immediately with the dessert of your choice. This sauce goes particularly well with ice cream.

VARIATION

For **easy minty choc sauce**, use 100 g (31/2 oz) plain dark mint chocolate instead of plain dark chocolate. Finely chop 6 fresh mint leaves and add to the mint chocolate and evaporated milk mixture. Heat gently, stirring until the chocolate is melted.

CHOCOLATE

White Chocolate Mousse

SERVES 6–8

200 g (7 oz) white chocolate, chopped
4 tablespoons milk
12 cardamom pods
200 g (7 oz) silken tofu
50 g (2 oz) caster sugar
1 egg white
crème fraîche or natural yogurt, to serve
cocoa powder, for dusting

Put the chocolate and milk in a heatproof bowl and melt over a saucepan of barely simmering water.

To release the cardamom seeds, crush the pods using a pestle and mortar. Discard the pods and crush the seeds finely. Place the crushed cardamom seeds and the tofu in a blender or food processor with half of the sugar, then blend well to make a smooth paste. Turn the mixture into a large bowl.

Whisk the egg white in a separate clean bowl, until it forms soft peaks. Gradually whisk in the remaining sugar.

Beat the melted chocolate mixture into the tofu until completely combined. Using a large metal spoon, fold in the whisked egg white.

Spoon the mousse into small coffee cups or glasses and chill in the fridge for at least 1 hour before serving. Serve topped with spoonfuls of crème fraîche or yogurt and a light dusting of cocoa powder.

VARIATION

For **white chocolate and Amaretto pots**, make the mousse mixture as above, omitting the cardamom and adding 2 tablespoons Amaretto liqueur when blending the tofu. Complete the recipe and chill as above. Serve with fresh raspberries instead of the crème fraîche or yogurt and cocoa powder.

Chocolate Mousse

SERVES 4–6

225 g (7½ oz) 70% cocoa vegan dark chocolate, plus extra to serve (optional)
150 ml (¼ pint) chickpea liquid (aquafaba)
150 g (5 oz) caster sugar
½ teaspoon salt

Melt the chocolate in a microwave in 30-second bursts or in a heatproof bowl over a pan of just-boiled water (don't let the bowl touch the water). Set aside to cool, but don't allow it to set.

Drain a can of chickpeas and measure the liquid – the amount you get varies from brand to brand, so measure it out and then use the same amount of sugar.

Put the chickpea liquid and sugar in a bowl and, using a hand whisk or stand mixer, begin to whisk. After 5 minutes, add the salt. It should take 10–12 minutes to get the mixture to form stiff peaks.

Carefully fold in the cooled, melted chocolate using a large metal spoon, if you have one. Divide the mixture between 4–6 ramekins or glasses, or put the whole lot in a big bowl and get people to dig in.

Grate chocolate on top, if you like, and allow to set at room temperature for at least 2 hours.

TIP

These have only four ingredients! Whisking up the liquid from a can of chickpeas gives you airy, fluffy, light puddings that only take 10 minutes to whip up, and the recipe is waste-free because you can use the chickpeas for Chickpea Tabbouleh (see page 73).

Chocolate Fudge Brownie

SERVES 8

200 g (7 oz) butter
200 g (7 oz) plain dark chocolate, chopped
175 g (6 oz) soft dark brown sugar
150 g (5 oz) caster sugar
4 eggs, beaten
50 g (2 oz) ground almonds
75 g (3 oz) plain flour
vanilla ice cream, to serve (optional)

Melt the butter and chocolate in a shallow ovenproof dish, about 23 cm (9 inches) across, over a low heat. Remove from the heat and leave to cool for a couple of minutes.

Beat together the sugars and eggs in a bowl, then stir in the chocolate mixture followed by the almonds and flour.

Wipe the rim of the ovenproof dish with a damp piece of kitchen paper to neaten, then pour in the chocolate mixture. Bake in a preheated oven, 180°C (350°F), Gas Mark 4, for 25 minutes, or until just set. Serve warm with vanilla ice cream, if liked.

Chocolate & Marshmallow Torte

SERVES 8

200 g (7 oz) plain dark chocolate, broken into pieces
100 g (3½ oz) unsalted butter
5 eggs, separated
175 g (6 oz) caster sugar
2 tablespoons plain flour, sifted
½ teaspoon ground cinnamon
2 tablespoons warm water
300 ml (½ pint) double cream
125 g (4 oz) vegan mini pink and white marshmallows

VARIATION

For **mixed nut torte**, fold in 100 g (31/2 oz) mixed pistachios, hazelnuts and almonds, roughly chopped, after the flour and cinnamon. Serve with 4 tablespoons toasted flaked almonds instead of the marshmallows.

Put the chocolate and butter in a bowl set over a saucepan of gently simmering water and leave to melt.

Whisk the egg whites in a large bowl until stiff, moist-looking peaks are formed, then gradually whisk in half the sugar, a teaspoonful at a time, until thick and glossy. Using the still dirty whisk, beat the egg yolks and remaining sugar in a third bowl until very thick.

Mix the warm chocolate and butter mixture gradually into the egg yolks. Stir in the flour and cinnamon, then loosen the mixture with the measured warm water. Gently fold in a spoonful of the meringue, then fold in the remainder.

Pour the mixture into a greased and base-lined 23 cm (9 inch) springform tin. Bake in a preheated oven, 180°C (350°F), Gas Mark 4, for 25–30 minutes until well risen and the top is crusty and the centre only just set. Leave to cool for 2 hours in the tin.

Remove the torte from the tin, discarding the lining paper. Cut into wedges. Softly whip the cream, then top wedges of torte with spoonfuls of cream and a sprinkling of marshmallows.

Choco Bread & Butter Pudding

SERVES 4

50 g (2 oz) unsalted butter, plus extra for greasing
4 chocolate croissants
50 g (2 oz) caster sugar
¼ teaspoon ground mixed spice
300 ml (½ pint) milk
4 eggs
1 teaspoon vanilla extract
icing sugar, to decorate
single cream, to serve

Grease a 1.2 litre (2 pint) shallow, round, ovenproof pie dish. Slice the croissants thickly and spread the butter over one side of each cut face of croissant. Stand the croissant slices upright and close together in the dish to completely fill it.

Mix the sugar and spice together, then spoon over the croissants and between the gaps. Stand the dish in a large roasting tin.

Beat the milk, eggs and vanilla extract together, then strain into the dish. Leave to stand for 15 minutes.

Pour hot water from the tap into the roasting tin to come halfway up the sides of the pie dish. Bake in a preheated oven, 180°C (350°F), Gas Mark 4, for about 25 minutes until the pudding is golden and the custard just set.

Lift the dish out of the roasting tin, dust with sifted icing sugar and serve the pudding warm with a little single cream.

VARIATION

For **fruited bread & butter pudding**, lightly butter 8 slices of white bread, cut into triangles and arrange in slightly overlapping layers in the dish, sprinkling with 75 g (3 oz) luxury dried fruit between the layers. Add the sugar as above, but omit the mixed spice. Mix the eggs, milk and vanilla, pour over the bread, then continue as above.

Creamy Vanilla Rice Pudding

SERVES 4

125 g (4 oz) pudding rice
about 750 ml (1¼ pints) whole milk
50 g (2 oz) caster sugar
1 teaspoon vanilla extract or 1 vanilla pod, split
25 g (1 oz) butter

Place all the ingredients in a saucepan and bring to the boil. Reduce the heat and simmer gently for 25–28 minutes, stirring frequently and adding more milk if necessary, until the rice is creamy and just tender.

Remove the vanilla pod, if using, spoon the rice pudding into bowls and serve immediately.

TIP

Any leftover rice pudding is delicious served cold with a handful of summer berries or with a dollop of homemade jam (see page 191), or simply dusted with cinnamon.

Syrup Sponge Pudding

££ · Veggie · <20

SERVES 6

175 g (6 oz) butter, softened, plus extra for greasing
175 g (6 oz) caster sugar
175 g (6 oz) self-raising flour
1 teaspoon baking powder
3 eggs
1 teaspoon vanilla extract
3 tablespoons milk
finely grated zest of ½ lemon
6 tablespoons golden syrup
cream or custard, to serve

Grease a 1.2 litre (2 pint) pudding basin with butter. Place all the ingredients, except the golden syrup, in a food processor and blend until smooth. Spoon 4 tablespoons of the golden syrup into the bottom of the prepared pudding basin, then add the pudding mixture and smooth the surface with a knife.

Cover with microwave-proof clingfilm and pierce the film a couple of times with a sharp knife. Cook in a microwave oven on medium heat for about 12 minutes. Test to see if it is cooked by inserting a skewer into the pudding; it should come out clean.

Leave to rest for 3 minutes, then turn out on to a deep plate and spoon over the remaining golden syrup. Serve warm with cream or custard.

Blackberry Crumble

£ · Veggie · >20

SERVES 4

750 g (1½ lb) blackberries
2 oranges, segmented
zest and juice of 1 orange
200 g (7 oz) butter
200 g (7 oz) plain flour
100 g (3½ oz) soft brown sugar
cream, ice cream or custard, to serve (optional)

Mix the blackberries, orange segments and the orange zest and juice together in a bowl.

In a separate bowl rub together the butter and flour with your fingertips until it resembles breadcrumbs and then stir in the sugar.

Tip the blackberry mixture into a large ovenproof dish and scatter over the crumble mixture to cover.

Bake in a preheated oven, 220°C (425°F), Gas Mark 7, for 20–25 minutes until golden. Remove from the oven and serve warm with cream, ice cream or custard, if liked.

Banana, Date & Walnut Loaf

££ · Veggie · >50

SERVES 10

400 g (13 oz) bananas, weighed with skins on
1 tablespoon lemon juice
300 g (10 oz) self-raising flour
1 teaspoon baking powder
125 g (4 oz) caster sugar
125 g (4 oz) butter, melted
2 eggs, beaten
175 g (6 oz) ready-chopped dried dates
50 g (2 oz) walnut pieces
walnut halves and banana chips, to decorate
  (optional)

Peel then mash the bananas with the lemon juice.

Put the flour, baking powder and sugar in a mixing bowl. Add the mashed bananas, melted butter and eggs and mix together. Stir in the dates and walnut pieces then spoon into a greased 1 kg (2 lb) loaf tin, its base and 2 long sides also lined with greased baking paper. Spread the surface level and decorate the top with walnut halves and banana chips, if using.

Bake in the centre of a preheated oven, 160°C (325°F), Gas Mark 3, for 1 hour 10 minutes–1¼ hours until well risen, the top has cracked and a skewer inserted into the centre comes out clean. Leave to cool for 10 minutes then loosen the edges, turn out on to a wire rack and peel off the lining paper. Leave to cool completely.

TIP
This loaf will keep for up to 5 days in an airtight container – if it lasts that long!

Earl Grey Lemon Drizzle Loaf

SERVES 8

vegan spread, for greasing
250 ml (8 fl oz) almond milk or other dairy-free milk
3 Earl Grey tea bags
110 ml (3¾ fl oz) flavourless oil
finely grated zest and juice of 2 lemons
300 g (10 oz) self-raising flour
225 g (7½ oz) caster sugar
pinch of salt

ICING

long strips of zest and juice of 1 lemon
100 g (3½ oz) icing sugar

Grease a 900 g (2 lb) loaf tin and use 2 strips of baking paper overlapping in a '+' shape to line the tin, which will help you to lift the loaf out when it's finished baking.

Put the almond milk and tea bags in a small saucepan and warm gently – you don't want to bring it to the boil, it should just be warm to the touch. Turn off the heat and stir well, pressing the tea bags against the side of the pan to infuse the milk with as much flavour as you can until it is a deep brown colour; this should take around 5 minutes. Discard the tea bags, making sure you squeeze all of the milk out of them first.

Add the oil, lemon zest and juice to the milk.

In a large bowl, whisk together the flour and sugar and salt, then slowly whisk in the wet ingredients, stirring well until you have a smooth batter.

Transfer the batter to the prepared tin. Bake in a preheated oven, 160°C (325°F), Gas Mark 3, for 50–55 minutes until a skewer inserted into the centre comes out clean. Leave to cool in the tin for 15 minutes before lifting out the loaf and transferring to a wire rack to cool fully.

To make the icing, slowly add the lemon juice to the icing sugar until you have a thick but spreadable icing – you may not need all the juice, because if your drizzle is too thin it will run off the loaf completely. Ice the top of the cake and top with long strips of lemon zest.

TIP

There's no cheaper way to add buckets of flavour to a cake than to use a few tea bags that you have lying around. Earl Grey and lemon work wonderfully together, and this loaf is so moist that it will keep in an airtight container for up to 7 days.

Apple Cake

SERVES 8

vegan spread, for greasing
350 g (11½ oz) self-raising flour
½ teaspoon bicarbonate of soda
½ teaspoon fine sea salt
1 teaspoon ground cinnamon (optional)
3–4 apples (total weight about 350 g/11½ oz),
    peeled, cored and chopped into 1–1.5 cm
    (½–¾ inch) chunks, plus extra (optional)
    for topping
75 g (3 oz) sultanas or raisins (optional)
50 g (2 oz) nuts, chopped (optional)
finely grated zest and juice of ½ lemon
75 ml (3 fl oz) flavourless oil
225 ml (7½ fl oz) dairy-free milk
2 tablespoons demerara sugar (optional)

Grease a 20 cm (8 inch) loose-bottomed cake tin and line the base with baking paper.

In a large bowl, combine the flour, bicarbonate of soda, salt and cinnamon, if using. Toss in the apple chunks, sultanas or raisins and nuts, if using, and coat them all thoroughly in the flour mixture.

In a smaller separate bowl, mix together the lemon zest and juice, oil and milk. Slowly add the wet ingredients to the dry and fold them in using a large spoon or spatula until fully combined.

Spoon the batter into the prepared tin, smoothing out the top. You can use one-quarter of an apple, very thinly sliced, laid out in a spiral shape on top of your cake, if you like. Sprinkle the demerara sugar over the top, if using, and bake in a preheated oven, 160°C (325°F), Gas Mark 3, for 1¼ hours until a skewer inserted into the centre comes out clean.

Allow to cool for 15 minutes in the tin before removing the sides of the loose-bottomed tin and popping the cake on to a wire rack. This is delicious served slightly warm, or will keep in an airtight container for up to 6 days.

TIP

This is the perfect way to use up any wrinkly apples, but it also works wonderfully with pears or rhubarb. Coating the fruit in the flour mixture makes sure it doesn't all sink to the bottom. The spices, fruit and nuts are optional – use whatever dried fruit and nuts you have.

Blueberry Bakewells

MAKES 18

125 g (4 oz) self-raising flour, plus extra for dusting
350 g (11½ oz) ready-made sweet shortcrust pastry
6 tablespoons blueberry jam
125 g (4 oz) slightly salted butter, softened
125 g (4 oz) caster sugar
2 eggs
½ teaspoon baking powder
1 teaspoon almond extract
100 g (3½ oz) ground almonds
4 tablespoons flaked almonds
75 g (3 oz) icing sugar, sifted

Roll out the pastry on a lightly floured surface and use to line a greased 28 x 18 cm (11 x 7 inch) shallow baking tin. Line the pastry case with baking paper and baking beans (or dried beans). Bake in a preheated oven, 200°C (400°F), Gas Mark 4, for 15 minutes. Remove the paper and beans and bake for a further 5 minutes. Reduce the oven temperature to 180°C (350°F), Gas Mark 4.

Spread the base of the pastry with the jam. Beat together the butter, caster sugar, eggs, flour, baking powder and almond extract in a bowl until smooth and creamy. Beat in the ground almonds. Spoon the mixture over the jam and spread gently in an even layer.

Scatter with the flaked almonds and bake for about 40 minutes until risen and just firm to the touch. Leave to cool in the tin.

Beat the icing sugar with a dash of water in a bowl to give the consistency of thin cream. Spread in a thin layer over the cake. Allow to set, then cut into squares or fingers.

TIP

For homemade blueberry jam, put 500 g (1 lb) fresh blueberries, 4 tablespoons lemon juice and 2 tablespoons water in a large saucepan and cook gently for about 8–10 minutes until the berries are soft. Stir in 450 g (14½ oz) preserving or granulated sugar and heat gently until the sugar dissolves. Bring to the boil and boil for 10–15 minutes until setting point is reached. Ladle into sterilized jars (see page 204), cover and label.

Raspberry Ripple Meringues

MAKES 12
40 g (1½ oz) fresh raspberries, plus extra
  to serve (optional)
2 tablespoons raspberry jam
4 egg whites
200 g (7 oz) caster sugar

Put the raspberries in a bowl and mash with a fork until broken up and turning juicy. Add the jam and mash together to make a purée. Tip into a sieve resting over a small bowl and press the purée with the back of a spoon to extract as much juice as possible.

Whisk the egg whites in a large clean bowl with a hand-held electric whisk until peaking. Whisk in a tablespoonful of the sugar and continue to whisk for about 15 seconds. Gradually add the remaining sugar, a spoonful at a time, until thick and glossy.

Drizzle over the raspberry purée and lightly stir in using a spatula or large metal spoon, scooping up the meringue from the base of the bowl so that the mixture is streaked with the purée. Do not to over-mix.

Drop large spoonfuls of the mixture, each about the size of a small orange, on to a large baking sheet lined with baking paper, then swirl with the back of a teaspoon. Bake in a preheated oven, 120°C (250°F), Gas Mark ½, for about 1¼ hours or until the meringues are crisp and come away easily from the paper. Leave to cool on the paper. Serve with extra raspberries, if liked.

Mango & Passion Fruit Trifle

SERVES 2
2 sponge fingers
75 ml (3 fl oz) Greek yogurt
100 ml (3 ½ fl oz) crème fraîche
2 passion fruit
½ ripe mango, peeled, pitted and diced

Break each sponge finger into 4 pieces and divide between 2 glasses. Mix the yogurt and crème fraîche together in a bowl.

Halve the passion fruit and scoop out the pulpy seeds. Spoon two-thirds of the seeds over the sponge fingers, then add half of the mango pieces.

Spoon half of the crème fraîche mixture over the fruit, then top with the remaining mango. Spoon over the remaining crème fraîche mixture and top with the remaining passion fruit seeds. Chill in the fridge for 1 hour before serving.

Melon & Mint Granita

SERVES 4–6

1 small watermelon (about 500 g/1 lb), peeled and deseeded
80 g (3¼ oz) caster sugar
80 ml (3½ fl oz) water
2 mint sprigs, plus extra to serve
3 tablespoons lime juice, or to taste

TIP

Use any flavoured liquid you like: lemon, apple or mango juice, or the leftover liquid from poached fruit. You can also blend any other fruit, such as canteloupe melon or strawberries, to a purée, then pass it through a sieve and use that as your flavoured base. Any spare melon juice can be kept in a bottle in the refrigerator for up to 4 days.

Blitz the melon in a food processor until smooth. Pass the purée through a sieve, discarding any fibres that won't pass through.

In a small saucepan, heat the sugar and measured water with the mint sprigs and stir until the sugar is dissolved, then boil for exactly 3 minutes (if you have a sugar thermometer, the syrup should reach 105°C/221°F). Discard the mint sprigs.

Mix 500 ml (17 fl oz) of the melon purée with the sugar syrup and season to taste with lime juice, remembering that the flavours should be strong because – when frozen – they will be muted.

Pour the mixture into a shallow freezerproof and airtight container or tray and leave to cool to room temperature, then freeze for 2–3 hours. After 1 hour, stir and scrape the granita with a fork to agitate the ice crystals forming. Do this every 30 minutes for a further 1–2 hours (the time it takes will depend on your freezer). You should be left with a crunchy, slushy mixture that should be served straight from the freezer with mint sprigs. You can also blitz the mixture in a food processor for a smoother 'slushy snow' texture.

Crunchy Berry Brûlée

SERVES 4

250 g (8 oz) mascarpone cheese
300 ml (½ pint) ready-made fresh custard
150 g (5 oz) mixed berries
100 g (3½ oz) caster sugar
1½ tablespoons water

Beat the mascarpone in a bowl until smooth. Gently stir in the custard. Transfer the mixture to a serving dish and scatter the berries over the top.

Place the sugar and measured water in a small heavy-based saucepan and slowly bring to the boil, carefully swirling the pan from time to time. Keep cooking until the sugar dissolves, then turns a deep caramel colour. Pour over the berries and leave for a few minutes to harden.

Banoffee Pie

££ Veggie <20

SERVES 4

200 g (7 oz) amaretti biscuits, lightly crushed
100 g (3½ oz) unsalted butter, melted
397 g (13 oz) can caramel
3 bananas, sliced
200 ml (7 fl oz) double cream
30 g (1¼ oz) plain dark chocolate, grated

Place the crushed amaretti biscuits in a bowl, pour over the melted butter and mix well.

Pour the buttered crumbs into a 20 cm (8 inch) loose-bottomed flan tin and press them into the base and sides. Chill for 10 minutes.

Spread the caramel over the biscuit base, then top with the sliced bananas.

Whip the cream to soft peaks and spread over the bananas. Scatter the grated chocolate over the top.

EASY TASTY CHEAP

Tiramisu

££££ · Veggie · >20

SERVES 4
200 ml (7 fl oz) double cream
50 ml (2 fl oz) Marsala wine
250 g (8 oz) mascarpone cheese
4 tablespoons icing sugar
1 teaspoon vanilla extract
300 ml (½ pint) very strong coffee, cooled
20 sponge fingers
25 g (1 oz) plain dark chocolate, grated,
  to decorate

Whip the cream in a bowl until stiff peaks form. Reserve 1 tablespoon of the Marsala, then stir the remaining Marsala into the cream with the mascarpone, 3 tablespoons of the icing sugar and the vanilla extract.

Stir the remaining Marsala and icing sugar into the coffee, then dip 4 of the sponge fingers into the mixture and place each in the bottom of a glass or small serving dish. The sponge fingers should be just soft, not soggy.

Spoon some of the creamy mixture on top, then repeat the layers to use up the remaining ingredients. Chill in the fridge for 20 minutes, then serve sprinkled with grated chocolate.

basics

Vegetable Stock

1 tablespoon sunflower oil
2 onions, roughly chopped
2 carrots, roughly chopped
2 celery sticks, roughly chopped
500 g (1 lb) mixture of other prepared fresh
   vegetables (such as parsnips, fennel, leeks,
   courgettes, mushrooms and tomatoes)
1.5 litres (2½ pints) water
a few herb sprigs, such as thyme or rosemary,
   or a couple of bay leaves
1 teaspoon black peppercorns

Heat the oil in a large, heavy-based saucepan and gently fry all the vegetables for 5 minutes.

Add the water, herbs and peppercorns, bring slowly to the boil. Reduce the heat and simmer the stock very gently for 40 minutes, skimming the surface from time to time if necessary.

Strain the stock through a large sieve. Don't squeeze the juice out of the vegetables or the stock will be cloudy. Leave the stock to cool completely, then chill.

FOR FISH STOCK

Melt 15 g (½ oz) butter in a large saucepan and gently fry 1 kg (2 lb) white fish bones and trimmings until the trimmings have turned opaque. Add a quartered onion, 2 roughly chopped celery sticks, a handful of parsley, several lemon slices and 1 teaspoon peppercorns. Cover with cold water and bring to a gentle simmer. Cook very gently for 30–35 minutes. Strain through a sieve and leave to cool. Cover and chill for up to 2 days or freeze for up to 3 months.

FOR CHICKEN STOCK

Place 1 large chicken carcass or 500 g (1 lb) chicken bones in a large saucepan and add 2 halved, unpeeled onions, 2 roughly chopped carrots, 1 roughly chopped celery stick, several bay leaves and 1 teaspoon black or white peppercorns. Just cover with cold water and bring to a gentle simmer. Reduce the heat to its lowest setting and cook, uncovered, for 2 hours. Strain through a sieve and leave to cool. Cover and store in the fridge for up to several days or freeze for up to 6 months.

Gravy

pan juices from roasted meat
1 tablespoon plain flour (less for a thin gravy)
300–400 ml (10–14 fl oz) liquid (this could
   be water, drained from the accompanying
   vegetables; stock; half stock and half water;
   or half wine and half water)
salt and pepper

Tilt the flameproof roasting tin used for your roast meat and skim off the fat from the surface with a large serving spoon until you are left with the pan juices and just a thin layer of fat.

Over a medium heat on the hob, sprinkle the flour into the tin and stir with a wooden spoon, scraping up all the residue, particularly from around the edges of the tin.

Gradually pour the liquid into the tin, stirring well until the gravy is thick and glossy. Let the mixture bubble, then check the seasoning, adding a little salt and pepper if necessary.

Cheat's Sourdough

MAKES 1 LARGE LOAF

450 g (14½ oz) strong white bread flour, plus extra for dusting
50 g (2 oz) strong wholemeal bread flour
10 g (2 teaspoons) fine sea salt
scant ⅛ teaspoon fast-action dried yeast
1 teaspoon white wine vinegar
375 ml (13 fl oz) cold water

Put the flours, salt, yeast, vinegar and measured water in a large bowl and mix well until fully combined. Cover with a damp tea towel and leave at room temperature to prove overnight (12 hours).

The next morning, the dough should have risen and be bubbly. Preheat the oven as high as it can go (240°C/475°F, Gas Mark 9) and place a large cast-iron casserole dish in the oven to preheat for at least 1 hour.

Meanwhile, lightly dust a work top with flour. Wet your hands and scrape out the dough from the bowl. On the work top, fold the 4 corners of the dough inwards to the centre, then flip the dough over. Using both hands, cup the dough and pull it in a clockwise motion to create tension on the surface and help form it into a round shape. It is a very wet dough, so don't worry if you don't get the hang of it at first as it will still bake beautifully. Once you're satisfied that you have a smooth top, leave the dough uncovered for 30 minutes to rest.

After 30 minutes, lightly flour the surface of the dough and the work top and flip the dough over. Pull out the corners to make a rough square, then fold the left third of the dough into the middle, then the right third on top of that. Roll the dough up tightly, and place seam-side down on a large piece of baking paper – the surface should be smooth on top. Use a sharp knife to score the top.

Lower the loaf on its paper into the casserole dish, cover and bake for 30 minutes, then remove the lid and bake for a further 20 minutes until deep golden and hollow sounding when tapped on the base. Place the loaf on a wire rack to cool. Leave for 1 hour before slicing.

Basic Pizza Dough

SERVES 4

7 g (¼ oz) fresh yeast or 1 teaspoon dried yeast
pinch of caster sugar
500 g (1 lb) plain flour, plus extra for dusting
350 ml (12 fl oz) lukewarm water
1½ teaspoons salt
olive oil, for oiling

Dissolve the yeast in a bowl with the sugar, 2 tablespoons of the flour and 50 ml (2 fl oz) of the measured water. Leave to stand for 5 minutes until it starts to form bubbles.

Add the remaining water, the salt and half the remaining flour and stir with one hand until you have a paste-like mixture. Gradually add all the remaining flour, working the mixture until you have a moist dough. Shape the dough into a ball, cover with a moist tea towel and leave to rest in a warm place for 5 minutes.

Lightly dust a work surface with flour and knead the dough for 10 minutes, or until smooth and elastic. Shape into 4 equal-sized balls and place, spaced apart, on a lightly oiled baking sheet. Cover with a moist tea towel and leave to rise in a warm place for 1 hour. Use according to your recipe.

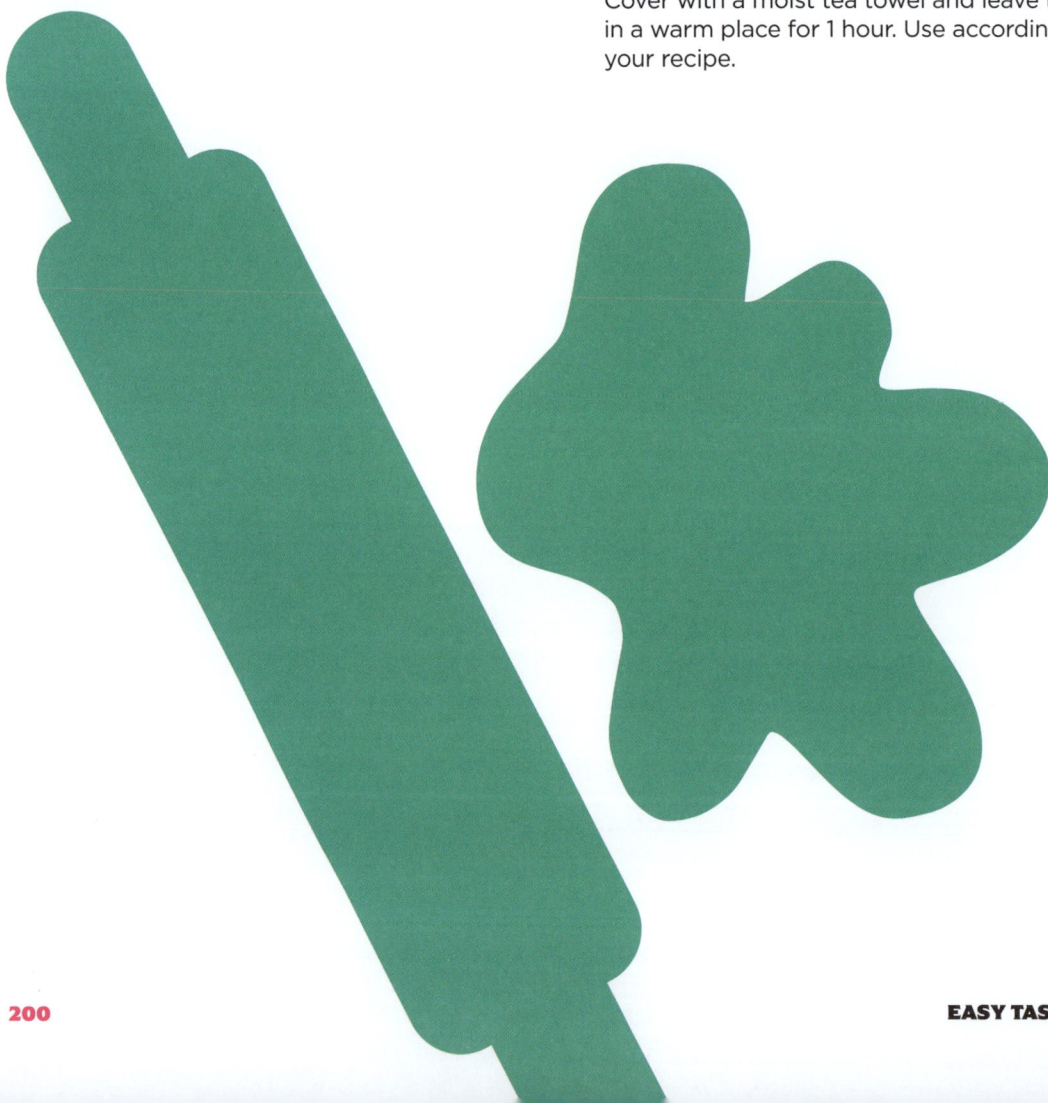

Homemade Pizza Dough

MAKES 4 THIN CRUST OR 3 THICK CRUST PIZZA BASES

400 g (13 oz) strong white bread flour
1 teaspoon salt
1 teaspoon fast-action dried yeast
1 tablespoon olive oil, plus extra for oiling
200–250 ml (7–8 fl oz) lukewarm water
2 tablespoons semolina (optional)
toppings of your choice

In a large bowl, combine the flour, salt, yeast and olive oil. Gradually add the measured water until you have a sticky, but not too wet, dough. Knead on a lightly oiled table – or in the bowl of a stand mixer – until smooth, elastic and springy (this will take 8–10 minutes). Leave the ball of dough in a lightly oiled bowl, covered with a tea towel, until doubled in size (about 1 hour). You can also leave it in the refrigerator overnight for a slower rise.

When you're ready to make your pizzas, preheat the grill to its highest possible setting. Also start to preheat an ovenproof frying pan over a medium-high heat.

Divide the dough into 3 for slightly thicker pizzas or 4 for thin. Roll each piece of dough into a ball, then use either a rolling pin or your hands to push it out into a circle as wide as the base of the pan (probably 20–25 cm/8–10 inches), keeping the edges a little thicker. If your dough resists being stretched, leave it covered with a tea towel for 5 minutes to relax, then come back to it. You shouldn't need any flour on the table to do this, as the dough contains oil.

Sprinkle a little semolina into your frying pan for an extra-crunchy base or leave it out if you don't have any. Carefully place a pizza base in the pan – the pan will be hot.

Add your chosen toppings to your pizza base in the pan – see pages 103–5.

When you're ready, put the pizza on the highest shelf underneath the grill for 5–6 minutes until the toppings are cooked through and the crust is golden and starting to get slightly charred. Repeat to cook the remaining pizzas.

TIP

This dough recipe is enough for when you have a few friends over, though it also halves and doubles very easily. You're going to need a frying pan or skillet that can go straight from the hob to the oven (no plastic or wood!) to make sure you get a crunchy bottom and a blistered golden top.

Taco Night Tortillas

MAKES 12–16

200 g (7 oz) masa harina (see tip), plus extra for dusting or as needed
¼ teaspoon salt
2 tablespoons vegetable oil
175 ml (6 fl oz) hot water, plus extra if needed

Combine the masa harina and salt in a large bowl and add the oil. Pour in the measured water in a steady stream and mix everything together with your hands.

Knead the dough in the bowl for 5–8 minutes until it feels smooth but firm. Masa is gluten-free, so it won't knead like a traditional bread dough – if it seems too dry and crumbly, add a little more hot water, or if it is too wet add more flour.

Wrap tightly in clingfilm and allow to rest at room temperature for at least 30 minutes and up to 5 hours.

Divide the dough into 12–16 pieces, depending on the size you'd like, and roll each piece into a ball. Choose 1 ball (cover the rest) and place it between the 2 sheets of a split freezer bag (this works better than clingfilm, which is a bit wrinkly) or baking paper. Roll out with a rolling pin, or use a heavy-based saucepan or casserole dish to push the ball out into a thin circle. (If the tortilla doesn't roll off the plastic easily it's probably too wet. Add a little extra flour and rest again for 30 minutes.)

Cook the tortilla in a hot, dry frying pan for 1–2 minutes on each side until brown spots start to appear.

Shape and fry the remaining tortillas, one at a time. (Because they are gluten-free, they need to go straight from being pressed into the pan or they will be hard to handle.) Keep them warm, wrapped in a tea towel, until they are all ready to serve. Store, wrapped in clingfilm, at room temperature for up to 2 days.

TIP

These tortillas can be cooked ahead of time and reheated when you need them. You can try baking them moulded over an upturned muffin tray to make little bowls or they're wonderful deep-fried as tostadas. Masa harina is ground maize flour and is not expensive at all, but you can swap it for plain flour if you can't find any.

Béchamel Sauce

SERVES 4

50 g (2 oz) butter
40 g (1½ oz) plain flour
300 ml (½ pint) milk
300 ml (½ pint) single cream, or use 600 ml
  (1 pint) milk in total and omit the cream
freshly grated nutmeg, to taste
salt and pepper

Melt the butter over a medium heat in a small, heavy-based saucepan. Stir in the flour and cook gently for 1–2 minutes, stirring to make a smooth paste.

Remove the pan from the heat and add the milk (very gradually to avoid lumps forming), continuously whisking or beating well with a wooden spoon. When all the milk is combined you should have a smooth sauce.

Stir in the cream or additional milk, a little nutmeg and salt and pepper and then return the pan to the heat. Cook gently, stirring well, for about 2 minutes until the sauce is smooth and thickened. Serve immediately.

Fresh Tomato Sauce

SERVES 4

1 kg (2 lb) very ripe, full-flavoured tomatoes
100 ml (3 ½ fl oz) olive oil
1 onion, finely chopped
2 garlic cloves, crushed
2 tablespoons chopped oregano
sprinkling of caster sugar (optional)
salt and pepper

Put the tomatoes in a heatproof bowl, cover with boiling water and leave for about 2 minutes or until the skins start to split. Pour away the water. Skin and roughly chop the tomatoes.

Heat the oil in a large, heavy-based saucepan and gently fry the onion for 5 minutes or until softened but not browned. Add the garlic and fry for a further 1 minute.

Add the tomatoes and cook, stirring frequently, for 20–25 minutes or until the sauce is thickened and pulpy.

Stir in the oregano and season to taste with salt and pepper. If the sauce is very sharp, add a sprinkling of caster sugar, if liked.

TIP

This is a good sauce to make in large quantities if you have a glut of tomatoes and can be frozen in small freezer bags or plastic containers. Canned tomatoes make a good alternative if the only fresh ones available don't look very appetizing. Substitute two 400 g (13 oz) cans of chopped tomatoes and cook until pulpy.

Confit Tomatoes

FILLS A 1 kg (2 lb) JAR
750 g (1½ lb) tomatoes, halved
1 garlic bulb, halved
a few thyme, oregano, basil or rosemary sprigs (optional)
350–500 ml (12–17 fl oz) olive oil
salt and pepper

Put the tomatoes into a snug-fitting, deep baking tray, placing them cut-sides up as this stops the liquid from the tomatoes leaching into the oil. Add the halved garlic bulb, preferably placing it cut-side down so it infuses the oil with more garlic flavour. Season well and add the herbs, if using.

Pour the olive oil over the tomatoes until it reaches halfway up the sides of the tray, then pop them in a preheated oven, 120°C (250°F), Gas Mark ½, for 1½–2 hours until the whole house smells amazing and the tomatoes have shrivelled and softened.

Allow to cool. Meanwhile, sterilize a jar by cleaning it thoroughly in hot soapy water, then putting it in a moderate oven preheated to 150°C (300°F), Gas Mark 2 for 10 minutes to dry. Rubber jar seals should not go in the oven; instead, place them in a bowl and cover with boiling water to sterilize.

Decant the cooled tomatoes into the sterilized jar. They will keep well at room temperature for up to 1 month.

TIP
A great way to use up any wrinkly, forgotten tomatoes and to make yourself a delicious flavoured oil using the cheapest base oil that you can get your hands on. The tomatoes keep for ages and you can use their garlicky, rich oil any time you're making a savoury base – in Marinara Sauce (see page 105) or in Bolognese (see page 206), for example. The measurements here are just a guide – you don't need to make this much or you can make more. All you need is some tomatoes in a snug-fitting container with enough oil to come halfway up their sides. Eat as a topping on toast or pizza, add to a salad or reheat as a quick pasta sauce.

Bolognese Sauce

SERVES 4

15 g (½ oz) butter
3 tablespoons olive oil
1 large onion, finely chopped
1 celery stick, finely chopped
1 carrot, finely chopped
3 garlic cloves, crushed
500 g (1 lb) lean minced beef
150 ml (¼ pint) red wine
2 x 400 g (13 oz) cans chopped tomatoes
2 tablespoons sun-dried tomato paste
3 tablespoons chopped oregano
3 bay leaves
salt and pepper
grated Parmesan cheese, to serve (optional)

Melt the butter with the oil in a large, heavy-based saucepan and gently fry the onion for 5 minutes. Add the celery and carrot and fry gently for a further 2 minutes.

Stir in the garlic, then add the minced beef. Fry gently, breaking up the meat, until lightly browned.

Add the wine and let the mixture bubble until the wine reduces slightly. Stir in the chopped tomatoes, tomato paste, oregano and bay leaves and bring to the boil.

Reduce the heat and cook very gently, uncovered, for about 45 minutes, stirring occasionally, until the sauce is very thick and pulpy. Remove the bay leaves. Check and adjust the seasoning, then serve with grated Parmesan, if liked.

Parsley Sauce

SERVES 4

15 g (½ oz) parsley (choose really fresh, fragrant parsley)
250 ml (8 fl oz) Vegetable Stock or Fish Stock (see page 197)
25 g (1 oz) butter
25 g (1 oz) plain flour
250 ml (8 fl oz) milk
3 tablespoons single cream
salt and pepper

Discard any tough stalks from the parsley and put it into a blender or food processor or blender with half of the stock. Blend until the parsley is very finely chopped.

Melt the butter over a medium heat in a heavy-based saucepan until bubbling. Tip in the flour and stir quickly to combine. Cook the mixture gently, stirring constantly with a wooden spoon, for 2 minutes.

Remove the pan from the heat and gradually whisk in the parsley-flavoured stock, then the remaining stock, until smooth. Whisk in the milk. Return to the heat and bring to the boil, stirring. Season with salt and pepper. Reduce the heat and continue to cook the sauce for about 5 minutes, stirring frequently, until it is smooth and glossy. The sauce should thinly coat the back of the spoon.

Stir in the cream and a little salt and pepper (remembering that if you've used ham stock, it might already be quite salty) and heat gently to warm through.

Basic Vinaigrette

SERVES 2

½ shallot, finely chopped

2 tablespoons vinegar (white wine vinegar, red wine vinegar or apple cider vinegar)

1 tablespoon Dijon mustard

3 tablespoons extra virgin olive oil or regular olive oil

1–2 teaspoons maple syrup or sugar

salt and pepper

Whisk together the shallot, vinegar and mustard. Slowly drizzle in the oil, whisking constantly until the vinaigrette has thickened and emulsified.

Season to taste with maple syrup or sugar, salt and pepper.

TIP

It's a great way of learning how to balance the acidity, saltiness and sweetness: the ratios of vinegar to oil to sweetener will vary depending on the brand or type of ingredient you're using, so taste regularly until you're happy that the dressing is delicate, sharp, ever so slightly sweet and salty.

Pesto

SERVES 4

50 g (2 oz) fresh basil, including stalks

50 g (2 oz) pine nuts

65 g (2½ oz) grated Parmesan-style cheese

2 garlic cloves, chopped

125 ml (4 fl oz) olive oil

salt and pepper

Tear the basil into pieces and put it into a blender or food processor with the pine nuts, cheese and garlic.

Process lightly until the nuts are broken into small pieces, scraping the mixture down from the sides of the bowl if necessary.

Add the oil and a little salt and pepper and blend to form a thick paste. Stir into freshly cooked pasta or turn into a bowl, cover and refrigerate. It can be kept, covered, for up to 5 days.

VARIATION

To make red pesto, drain 125 g (4 oz) sun-dried tomatoes in oil, chop them into small pieces and add to the food processor instead of the basil.

Breadcrumb Pesto

£ Vegan

<20

MAKES 350 G (11½ OZ)

30 g (1¼ oz) breadcrumbs, toasted if fresh

30 g (1¼ oz) any raw nuts or an extra 30 g (1¼ oz) breadcrumbs

large handful of spinach (about 40 g/1½ oz)

large handful of basil (about 40 g/1½ oz)

finely grated zest and juice of 1 lemon

1 garlic clove

4 tablespoons extra virgin olive oil

3–4 tablespoons cold water

salt and pepper

Whizz all the ingredients together in a food processor until smooth, adding as much of the measured water as you need to loosen the pesto. Season with salt and pepper to taste.

Keep in an airtight container in the refrigerator for up to 2 weeks.

TIP

The single best thing you can do with leftover herbs is to blitz them into a pesto.

Miso Sesame Dressing

£ Vegan

<20

SERVES 2

2 tablespoons flavourless oil

2 tablespoons sesame oil

1 tablespoon lime juice

1 tablespoon miso paste

1 tablespoon soy sauce

1–2 teaspoons maple syrup or sugar

salt and pepper

Whisk all the ingredients together and season with salt and pepper to taste.

TIP

Great tossed with warm roasted vegetables – they soak up lots of the savoury flavour – and good over raw spinach and cucumber, served as a cooling side dish.

Maple Mustard Dressing

£ · Vegan · <20

SERVES 2

4 tablespoons olive oil
2 tablespoons white wine vinegar
1 tablespoon maple syrup
1 tablespoon wholegrain mustard
1 teaspoon Dijon mustard
salt and pepper

Whisk all the ingredients together and season with salt and pepper to taste.

TIP
An equivalent to a honey-mustard dressing, that just happens to save the bees.

Garlic & Chive Vinaigrette

£ · Vegan · <20

SERVES 2

2 tablespoons red wine vinegar
1 garlic clove, finely chopped
1 tablespoon finely chopped chives
3 tablespoons extra virgin olive oil or regular olive oil
1–2 teaspoons maple syrup or sugar
salt and pepper

Whisk together the vinegar, garlic and chives. Slowly drizzle in the oil, whisking constantly until the vinaigrette has thickened and emulsified.

Season to taste with maple syrup or sugar, salt and pepper.

TIP
Wonderful with chopped salads and green vegetables, plus this is also rather nice to use as a dip for your pizza crusts.

Jalapeño & Lime Dressing

£ · Vegan · <20

SERVES 2

2 tablespoons finely chopped pickled jalapeños
finely grated zest and juice of 1 lime
2 tablespoons flavourless oil
2 tablespoons finely chopped coriander
1–2 teaspoons maple syrup or sugar
salt and pepper

Whisk all the ingredients together and season with salt and pepper to taste.

TIP
If you have a half-eaten jar of pickled jalapeños lingering in the refrigerator, make a batch of this dressing and toss it through a sweetcorn and black bean salad, or serve over a simple tossed salad with lettuce and avocado for an instant hit of Mexican flavour.

Any Can Hummus

SERVES 6

400 g (13 oz) can chickpeas or any other canned bean
¼ teaspoon bicarbonate of soda
4 tablespoons tahini
2–3 tablespoons lemon juice
1 teaspoon ground cumin
1 garlic clove, grated
salt and pepper

TO SERVE (OPTIONAL)

extra virgin olive oil or regular olive oil
chilli flakes

Put the chickpeas, or other beans, and their liquid into a small saucepan with the bicarbonate of soda. Bring to the boil, then reduce the heat to a simmer and cook for 15 minutes until extremely tender.

Drain the chickpeas, reserving the liquid.

Blitz the chickpeas with the tahini, 2 tablespoons of the lemon juice, the cumin and garlic until smooth, adding 4–5 tablespoons of the reserved liquid from the saucepan, until incredibly smooth and creamy. Season to taste, adding the remaining lemon juice if you want it.

Serve, drizzled with olive oil and chilli flakes, if you like.

TIP

The trick to smooth hummus is to recook the canned beans with bicarbonate of soda until they are incredibly tender. No need for the traditional and very laborious peeling of the chickpea skins, yet no grainy dips in sight – life changing.

Hot & Smoky Hummus with Warm Flatbread

SERVES 4

400 g (13 oz) can chickpeas, rinsed and drained
3 tablespoons lemon juice
1 large garlic clove, crushed
2 tablespoons tahini
1 teaspoon hot smoked paprika, plus extra
  for sprinkling
½ teaspoon ground cumin
150 ml (¼ pint) extra virgin olive oil, plus extra
  for drizzling
2 tablespoons sesame seeds
salt and pepper

TO SERVE

4 Lebanese or Turkish flatbreads
  crunchy raw vegetable crudités (optional)

Put all the ingredients, except the olive oil, sesame seeds and salt and pepper in a blender or food processor and process until smooth. With the machine still running, very slowly drizzle the oil into the chickpea paste until it is all completely incorporated. Season to taste with salt and pepper and then scrape the hummus into a small dish.

Heat a dry, nonstick frying pan and toast the sesame seeds over a medium-low heat, moving them quickly around the pan until they are golden brown. Stir most of the sesame seeds into the hummus, then sprinkle the rest over the top.

Wrap the flatbreads in foil and heat in a preheated oven, 160°C (325°F), Gas Mark 3, for about 10 minutes until warmed through. Drizzle the hummus with olive oil, sprinkle with smoked paprika and serve with the warm flatbreads and crunchy vegetable crudités, if liked.

Tomato Salsa

SERVES 6

400 g (13 oz) tomatoes, roughly chopped
1 garlic clove, grated
large handful of coriander, finely chopped
finely grated zest and juice of 2 limes
1 red chilli, deseeded and finely chopped
  (optional)
salt and pepper

Mix all the ingredients together and season to taste.

Guacamole

SERVES 4

2 ripe avocados, peeled, pitted and chopped
juice of 1 lime
6 cherry tomatoes, diced
1 tablespoon chopped fresh coriander
1–2 garlic cloves, crushed
oatcakes or vegetable crudités, to serve

Put the avocados and lime juice in a bowl and mash together to prevent discoloration, then stir in the remaining ingredients.

Serve immediately with oatcakes or vegetable crudités.

Avocado Crema

SERVES 6

2 avocados, peeled and pitted
3 tablespoons lime juice
salt and pepper

Put the avocados and lime juice into a blender and blitz until smooth, adding 1 tablespoon of water if needed. Season well.

Store with a strip of clingfilm pushed firmly and directly on the surface of the dip, to prevent it from browning.

TIP
Avocados have a bad 'expensive' reputation, but this easy dip makes an over- or under-ripe avocado into something delicious, and you only need a little to add a spot of luxury to your food.

Roasted Red Pepper Dip

SERVES 6

2 red peppers, halved, cored and deseeded
2 large tomatoes, halved
3 tablespoons olive oil
1 tablespoon sherry vinegar
1 garlic clove, roughly chopped
1 teaspoon smoked paprika
150 g (5 oz) stale bread, ripped into pieces
salt and pepper

Place the red peppers and tomatoes on a foil-lined baking tray, drizzle with 1 tablespoon of the oil, season and roast, in a preheated oven, 220°C (425°F), Gas Mark 7, for 35 minutes until blistered, slightly charred and soft.

Remove and discard the skins from the peppers and tomatoes once they're cooked and add the rest to a blender with the remaining olive oil, the sherry vinegar, garlic, paprika and bread. Blitz until you have a rough and chunky dip. Season to taste and serve.

TIP
This is essentially a traditional Spanish Romesco sauce, but without the expensive almonds of the classic version.

Baba Ghanoush

£ Vegan >20

SERVES 6

2 aubergines
1 garlic clove, grated
2 tablespoons tahini
2 tablespoons lemon juice
1 tablespoon extra virgin olive oil or regular olive oil, plus extra to serve
1 teaspoon maple syrup
pomegranate seeds, to serve (optional)
salt and pepper

TIP
This recipe is a great way to use up any wrinkly, forgotten-about aubergines.

If you have a gas hob, place the aubergines directly over the flame. Grill for 15–20 minutes, turning using tongs, until completely blistered and blackened and soft inside. (Alternatively, you can do this under the grill.)

Halve the aubergines and scoop out the flesh, discarding the blackened skins.

Finely chop the aubergine flesh and transfer to a bowl. Mix with the garlic, tahini, lemon juice, oil and maple syrup and season to taste. Top with a drizzle of olive oil to serve, adding pomegranate seeds, if you like.

This will keep in an airtight container in the refrigerator for up to 4 days.

Coriander & Parsley Zhoug

£ Vegan <20

MAKES 350 G (11½ OZ)

large handful of coriander (about 40 g/1½ oz)
large handful of parsley (about 40 g/1½ oz)
large handful of spinach (about 40 g/1½ oz)
finely grated zest and juice of 1 lemon
3 tablespoons extra virgin olive oil or regular olive oil
1 green chilli, seeds left in, roughly chopped
1 teaspoon ground cumin
1 teaspoon ground coriander
2–3 tablespoons cold water
salt and pepper

Whizz all the ingredients together in a food processor until smooth, adding as much of the measured water as you need to loosen the pesto. Season with salt and pepper to taste.

Keep in an airtight container in the refrigerator for up to 2 weeks.

TIP
Zhoug is a spicy Yemeni pesto. Gorgeously green and fiercely hot, use it to top any roasted vegetables to liven them up and serve alongside something cooling, such as Limey Cashew Cream (see page 86) or cucumber.

Vegan Parmesan

£ Vegan · <20

FILLS A 200 G (7 OZ) JAR

75 g (3 oz) cashew nuts, peanuts or
flaked almonds
3 tablespoons nutritional yeast
½ teaspoon salt

Whizz all the ingredients in a food processor until you have the texture of fine sand.

Pop in a jar and store at room temperature for up to 3 months.

TIP

Store-bought 'vegan cheese' is expensive, stinks the refrigerator out and is mainly just processed coconut oil. This cheats' version blitzes nuts with nutritional yeast and salt. It keeps in a jar for months and livens up pizzas, pasta and tarts with its salty savouriness.

Pea & Mint Pesto

£ Vegan · <20

MAKES 350 G (11½ OZ)

100 g (3½ oz) frozen peas, blanched in boiling
water for 1 minute, then drained
large handful of mint (about 30 g/1¼ oz)
large handful of spinach (about 40 g/1½ oz)
finely grated zest and juice of 1 lemon
3 tablespoons extra virgin olive oil or regular
olive oil
2–3 tablespoons cold water
salt and pepper

Whizz all the ingredients together in a food processor until smooth, adding as much of the measured water as you need to loosen the pesto. Season with salt and pepper to taste.

Keep in an airtight container in the refrigerator for up to 2 weeks.

TIP

Peas are cheaper than buckets of herbs and nuts and they lend a great hearty texture to this pesto, which is lovely alongside spring vegetables, such as asparagus, new potatoes and broad beans.

From croissants and quiches to pies and pasties, pastry should be a staple of every home – especially student ones. The easiest way to get started with this versatile and tasty dough is simply to buy it ready-made from a supermarket – there are loads of different types available to suit every budget, including vegetarian and vegan options. Getting to grips with pastry might appear daunting at first, but follow the steps below and you'll soon be a master of three of the most popular types and creating pastry-based meals that will wow your housemates.

Puff Pastry

Puff pastry doesn't need to be blind-baked. If making a puff pastry tart, roll it out and score 2 cm (1 inch) around the edge. Prick the centre of the pastry with a fork to help the edges puff up and the base to cook through without becoming soggy.

Preheat a baking tray while you preheat the oven to 190°C (375°F), Gas Mark 5. Sliding a puff pastry tart on to a hot baking sheet will give an instant hit of heat from below, so no soggy bottoms.

Brush the pastry with 1 tablespoon or so of milk (or a dairy-free alternative) on any exposed edges to help it to brown evenly.

Shortcrust Pastry

These pastry cases need to be blind-baked before filling. To do this, preheat the oven to 180°C (350°F), Gas Mark 4. Roll the pastry out to fit the chosen tin, prick it with a fork all over, then chill. Line the pastry case with a piece of nonstick baking paper and fill with baking beans or raw rice or dried beans. Bake for 15 minutes, until the pastry is sandy to the touch with no uncooked patches. Remove the baking paper and cook for a further 5 minutes until lightly golden, before adding your chosen filling.

It's easier to trim off any overhanging pastry after blind-baking and this also helps avoid the pastry shrinking during cooking. Use a serrated knife to trim the pastry edges while still warm.

Filo Pastry

Brush this with a little bit of oil between every layer to ensure you get flaky shards. Filo doesn't need to be blind-baked, but when it's in the oven you may sometimes need to cover it with foil to prevent it from browning too quickly.

It's quite show-stopping if you scrunch up filo pastry to top a pie filling, or you can use it to make spanakopita-style swirls.

Glossary

UK	US
Aubergine	Eggplant
Bacon rashers, back/streaky	Bacon slices, Canadian-style/normal
Baking paper/parchment	Parchment paper
Baking sheet	Cookie sheet
Barbecue	grill
Beans, broad/flageolet	Beans, butter/Great northern
Beetroot	Beets
Bicarbonate of soda	Baking soda
Biscuit	Cookie
Chickpea	Garbanzo bean
Chips (potato)	Fries (potato)
Clingfilm	Plastic wrap
Coriander	Cilantro (if referring to the fresh herb)
Cornflour	Cornstarch
Courgette	Zucchini
Cream, double/single	Cream, heavy/light
Dark chocolate	Semi-sweet chocolate
Dried chilli flakes	Crushed red pepper flakes
Electric whisk	Electric beaters
Flour, plain/strong/wholemeal	Flour, all-purpose/bread/whole-wheat
Flour, self-raising	Use all-purpose flour plus 1 teaspoon baking powder per 125 g (4 oz) of flour
Floury potatoes	Baking potatoes
Foil	Aluminum foil
Frying pan	Skillet
Gherkin	Pickle
Gram flour	Chickpea flour
Grill	Broil/broiler
Groundnut oil	Peanut oil
Hob	Stovetop
Icing	Frosting
Jam	Preserves
Jug	Pitcher
Kitchen paper	Paper towel
Mixed spice	Pie spice mix
Muslin	Cheese cloth
Natural yogurt	Plain yogurt
Passata	Sieved tomatoes
Pepper (green, red, yellow)	Bell pepper
Porridge oats	Rolled oats
Prawns (king)	Shrimp (jumbo)
Rapeseed oil	Canola oil
Rocket	Arugula
Scone	Biscuit
Sieve	Strainer
Shortcrust pastry	Basic pie dough
Spring onion	Scallion
Stem ginger	Preserved ginger
Stock	Broth
Suet	Shortening
Sugar, caster/icing/muscovado	Sugar, superfine/confectioners'/brown
Tomato purée	Tomato paste